TENERIFE

Compact Guide: Tenerife is the ultimate quick-reference guide to this classic destination. It tells you everything you need to know about the island's attractions: weird-looking volcanic landscapes, magnificent hiking routes, delicious local cuisine, breathtaking views across green forests and arid deserts, beautiful beaches, and last but not least, Mount Teide – the highest mountain in Spain.

This is just one title in *Apa Publications'* new series of pocket-sized, easy-to-use guidebooks intended for the independent-minded traveller. *Compact Guides* pride themselves on being up-to-date and authoritative. They are in essence mini travel encyclopedias, designed to be comprehensive yet portable, as well as readable and reliable.

Star Attractions

An instant reference
to some of Tenerife's
most popular tourist
attractions to help
you on your way.

Santa Cruz p18

Puerto de la Cruz p30

Parrot Park p32

Playa de las Américas
p34

Masca p38

Teide National Park
p45

La Laguna p49

Punta del Hidalgo p55

Candelaria
p63

San Juan de Rambla
p60

Playa de San Marcos
p61

Tenerife

Introduction

Places

Culture

Leisure

Practical Information

Tenerife – Island of Surprises

Landing by plane in Tenerife can be quite a shock for first-time visitors. Just as the plane touches down at the Reina Sofía airport, the newcomers look out of the window expectantly – and see an ochre-coloured wasteland of volcanic rock all round the airport, with nothing remotely reminiscent of the lush, fairytale holiday paradise they may have been expecting. The sun's shining, though, and the odd palm tree can be seen waving in the breeze.

The next shock for the first-time visitor is the seemingly infinite number of tourist ghettoes in and around Las Américas. It's almost as if someone were trying as hard as possible to put people off the island for good. But all this disappointment is concentrated into the first few hours of a holiday here. Things very soon improve, as any Tenerife *aficionado* will tell you – with each day you get to know the island a little bit better.

Tenerife's landscape is a combination of all the different natural scenery you can expect to find on any of the Canary Islands, and even more besides. It has eight different vegetation zones, with fertile mountain slopes and valleys, high desert, deep ravines, broad lava fields, tropical gardens, misty forests, remote hamlets, peaceful villages and exciting towns. The island's natural attractions begin with its numerous beaches and end at the top of the highest mountain in all Spain, the volcanic Mount Teide (3,717m/12,194ft). Tenerife isn't the kind of place with miles of deserted, sandy beach (those can usually be found out of season on Fuerteventura), but bathing and swimming are catered for all around the coast.

The very best way to experience the full beauty of Tenerife is to go on a hiking trip. Even though most places and sights can easily be reached by car – often to the annoyance of nature lovers – the most superb landscapes on the island can still only be properly appreciated on foot, during a hike. Don't expect not to meet anyone on the way, because you will; but the strange thing is that an increasing number of the people you'll encounter on hiking trips are *Tinerfeños*, many of whom only began discovering their island's real delights when the 'crazy' tourists started driving them inland.

The undisputed highlight of any hike of course is Mount Teide, situated inside Las Cañadas, one of the largest volcanic craters in the world. Standing out clearly against the deep blue of the sky, the mountain's summit is covered with snow even in summer. None of the other Canary Islands can compete with its sheer majesty. The weird moonscape up in Las Cañadas is also an experience that is definitely not to be missed, especially when the shadows grow longer towards dusk.

Life on the beach

5

Shady Icod de los Vinos

Location and size

Tenerife is part of the Spanish autonomous community of the Canary Islands and its 2,057 sq km (794 sq miles) make it the largest island in the archipelago – although it is actually around one fifth smaller than Luxembourg. The Canaries lie off the west coast of Africa, roughly on a level with southern Morocco. The archipelago comprises the islands of Lanzarote, Fuerteventura and Gran Canaria to the east, and Tenerife, La Gomera, La Palma and El Hierro to the west.

The nearest island to Tenerife is La Gomera, about 30km (18 miles) away. Gran Canaria is roughly twice as far to the southeast and the ocean between the two islands is over 2,000m (6,561ft) deep.

Tenerife's Mount Teide is not only the highest mountain in the Canaries but in all Spain as well. In clear weather almost all the other islands of the archipelago can be seen from its summit (Fuerteventura is usually rather hazy and Lanzarote only just peeks over the horizon).

6

In the holiday mood

Climate and when to go

Tenerife can be visited just about any time of year because of its moderate, spring-like climate in the coastal areas. The seasons and regional climatic differences are definitely noticeable higher up, however. The island has a windward and a leeward side, with the trade winds caressing the north of the island continuously from spring until autumn, creating a large expanse of cloud cover, and the sunny, leeward side is in the south.

The north, cooler and more moist, can be roughly divided up into three climatic zones: the land beneath the clouds, the land inside the clouds and the land above the clouds. Beneath the clouds, there is a warm subtropical climate all year round with many hours of sunshine and hardly any rain. The day and night temperatures differ by only a few degrees. Rain is more likely to fall in the late autumn and winter months, with up to a third of the entire annual precipitation falling in November alone.

The land inside the clouds lies roughly between 500m (1,640ft) and 1,200m (3,936ft) above sea level and is characterised by a higher degree of humidity, greater rainfall and far cooler summers. The sun usually only shines in the mornings. Here the earth absorbs the moisture that is so important for the rest of the island. Temperatures at night and during the winter are also a lot cooler than those in the coastal regions.

The land above the clouds experiences the sharpest fluctuations in temperature, not only between day and night but also summer and winter. In summertime the weather is warm and dry, and sometimes quite hot, but it gets very cold at night. In the winter it is relatively dry, but temperatures fall into the minuses. The odd blizzard can also occur, with the snow remaining on the ground for weeks. When this happens there are often small lakes in Las Cañadas formed by melted snow.

In the southern part of the island, clouds are generally rare. The sun shines longest here in both summer and winter, and rainfall is very infrequent. Those looking for all the sun they can get should thus opt for a holiday in southern Tenerife, while those keener on hiking and moderate temperatures would do better in the north, where the winters are cooler but not really all that cold (average annual temperature 18°C/64°F).

Geology and landscape

Like all the Canary Islands, Tenerife was formed by volcanic activity beneath the Atlantic Ocean. While the eastern islands appeared up to around 20 million years ago, the western ones including Tenerife were formed a lot later (eight to12 million years ago). Until around three million years ago there were probably just three islands consisting of the Anaga, the Teno Massif and the hills near Teje, and Valle San Lorenzo. They were melted into the Tenerife we know today during a gigantic volcanic process which created the island's mighty backbone, the Cumbre Dorsal, and its enormous central volcano. The original volcano probably never blew off its cone, but instead collapsed slightly back into itself, leaving behind one of the largest *calderas* (sunken craters) in the world, Las Cañadas. The oval crater measures 17km (10 miles) at its widest point, and its walls measured from the base exceed heights of 500m (1,640ft) in places.

Volcanic layers, Cumbre Dorsal

The last major volcanic activity on Tenerife occurred around 500,000 years ago. At first the Pico Viejo was flung up out of the valley of the original crater, and it later became today's Pico del Teide. The most recent eruption on Tenerife took place in 1909 on the Chinyero, just north of Santiago del Teide.

Punta del Teno and Masca Valley

Due to the island's volcanic past, there are comparatively few large flat areas on the island apart from Las Cañadas, which were used as summer grazing pastures for goats until quite recently. Alongside the high plain of La Laguna and the high valley of Santiago del Teide, there are several other, smaller *valles*: the northern Valle de Orotava with its southern offshoot Valle de Güímar, the Valle de Guerra in the northeast, and the Valle San Lorenzo in the southwest. The *valles* on Tenerife aren't valleys in the normal sense of the word, but rather rifts between the various mountain ridges, partially filled with eroded stone. Since the volcanic soil in these valleys is extremely fertile, most of the island's agriculture is based here.

Cacti grow on the dry slopes

Flora

Anyone with a poinsettia in a flowerpot at home will be amazed when they take a stroll through Tenerife's parks and hotel gardens to encounter its various tree-sized relations. Tenerife's tropical and subtropical plants, some native, some imported, are among the island's most attractive features. Several of the indigenous plants, including the legendary dragon tree, the cactus-like Pillar Euphorbia (candelabra cactus), the Canarian laurel and several types of Canarian fern, date from the Tertiary period and can only be found as fossils in other regions such as the Mediterranean.

Altitude and climate determine the different types of flora on the island. Down by the coast and extending to 600m (1,968ft) above sea level, one mainly sees cacti and succulents. The plants here are well adapted to absorbing the tiny amounts of rain that fall and save them up for longer periods of drought later on. The species of spurge known as euphorbia *(Euphorbia canariensis)* is widespread, and covers many of the dry slopes. The dragon tree *(Dracaena draco)*, which is related to the yucca, is one of the largest native trees, and another one commonly found in this zone is the most elegant palm tree of all, the *Phoenix canariensis*, which is related to the date-palm of North Africa and the Middle East, but has larger, more luxuriant leaves. It bears a small date-like fruit known as the *tamara*, which is, however, inedible.

Plants imported over the centuries from abroad include the prickly pear, the American agave, the famous Bird of Paradise plant, bougainvillea, hibiscus and oleander – many of them responsible for the luxuriant blossom in the island's avenues and parks. There are also lots of acacia, Indian laurel and eucalyptus, the scent of which almost makes you forget the traffic fumes in the busier parts.

Dragon tree

Juniper bushes are another feature of the warmer zone down near the south coast. Native laurel is confined to the north and grows in the cloud layer created by the trade winds. The Canarian laurel can grow up to 20m (65ft) in height and its leaves are used for culinary purposes. The Mercedes forest near La Laguna is one of the largest laurel forests on the island.

Pine forest on the Cumbre Dorsal

The pine forests begin at between 1,000m (3,280ft) and 2,000m (6,561ft) up. The Canary pine *(Pinus canariensis)* has particularly long needles and the moisture it stores is extremely important for the island's ecosystem. Near the pine layer are two more plants endemic to Tenerife: a gorse-like bush with white flowers known as *Cytisus proliferus*, and the rock rose *(Cistus symphitifolius)* with its pink flowers.

Plants in the subalpine zone are mostly to be found above the tree level, especially in Las Cañadas. The most distinctive plant – also called 'the pride of Tenerife' *(Orgullo di Tenerife)* – is the red Teide echium, which blooms from May to the beginning of July. The largest specimens of this threatened species can grow as high as 2m (6ft). Few other plants manage to survive in the desert-like, arid landscape up here but one which can is *retama*, the pink-and-white Teide broom *(Spartocytisus nubigens)*.

Delicate blooms

The most barren zone of all begins above 2,700m (8,858ft) in the shadow of the volcanic crater and the most famous plant up here is an inconspicuous violet *(Viola cheiranthifolia)*, known to the Spanish as Violeta del Teide. It blooms from early spring to early summer but unfortunately it is now on the endangered list.

Giant fern

Fauna

The wildlife on Tenerife is generally a lot less interesting than its flora. The largest wild mammals are moufflons, but they were imported as an attraction several years ago. Their population has swelled since then, and because they threaten the flora on Mount Teide the decision has now been taken to keep their numbers down, and some 50 animals are hunted each year. Rabbits, introduced in feudal times are hunted too, with the aid of tame ferrets and rifles. There are also several species of reptile, all harmless, including the gecko and the Canary lizard. The most famous bird is of course the canary. Only the male sings which is all it has in common with the popular cage bird, whose brightly coloured plumage was a result of breeding during the last century. The indigenous canary has a disappointing greyish-green colour.

As far as aquatic life is concerned, the sea around Tenerife teems with fish of all shapes and sizes, including dolphin and marlin, and fish is the staple diet of many coastal communities.

The population is growing steadily

Catholicism dominates

Guanche prince in Candelaria

Population and religion

As a result of the increase in tourism and prosperity, the population of Tenerife has been growing steadily over the past decades. At the last census there were 685,000 people living on the island, 60 percent of them in the catchment areas around the capital, Santa Cruz, and La Laguna. There are also around 100,000 long-term residents from abroad, mostly centred in the southwest and Puerto de la Cruz. The average tourist's stay is approximately ten days. Villages without any tourist infrastructure or agricultural advantages are losing their inhabitants – mostly young people – to the larger tourist areas, and several hamlets and farms in remote areas are now completely deserted.

The original cave-dwelling inhabitants were sun-worshippers and had their own pagan deities and rituals. Spanish supremacy made Roman Catholicism the only official religion, a situation that endured until the end of Franco's dictatorship. As in other parts of Spain, there are now large communities of Baptists, Mormons, Muslims, and Jehova's Witnesses besides the substantial body of Catholics.

Language

The official language on Gran Canaria is Spanish (*Castellano*). However, a strong local dialect is widely spoken; its main characteristics are the swallowing of final consonants, the increased use of the subjunctive and the adoption of South American vocabulary. Thus '*autobus*' becomes '*guagua*', and '*patata*' (potato) becomes '*papa*'. English and German are widely understood and spoken in tourist centres.

Ethnic origins

Tenerife's native population reflects the history of the archipelago as a whole. Most common are the descendants of the Spanish conquerors and the hispanicized Guanches, whose ancestors (*see page 15*) are widely thought to have had Northwest African tribal origins. All the trading and seafaring nations have made their contribution to the Canary Islanders' ethnic origins, too.

Economy

Before Tenerife was colonised, its inhabitants led a semi-nomadic existence, herding goats and cultivating cereal. Hunting animals with Stone Age weapons and fishing the island's shallow coastal waters provided extra sources of protein. Under Spanish rule the island's economy was adapted to suit the needs of the motherland. Broadly speaking, one monoculture succeeded another as the centuries progressed. An early phase during which people were taken away as slaves and the domestic animals served as fresh food for ship's crews was followed by the sugar-cane boom, when many pine forests were burnt to provide the heat needed for refining it. Wine cultivation on Tenerife lasted nearly three centuries until it came to an abrupt end with the advent of the grape virus phylloxera during the 1880s. In the mid-19th century there was a brief economic upswing thanks to the cochineal insect *(cochenille)*. This insect produces a kind of red dye which is still used today in the production of cosmetics, chemical preparations and alcoholic beverages. Another reason why cochineal production was so successful was because the insects' host plant, the prickly pear, also grows successfully in the areas of volcanic wasteland on Tenerife known as *malpaís* (literally 'badlands'). It was the advent of industrially produced chemical dyes that brought an end to the mini-boom.

Since then, the main product has been a particularly delicious dwarf banana. This was introduced from Indochina and subsequently marketed by the British a century ago. Until recently, up to 70 percent of Spain's bananas came from Tenerife. As far as quality is concerned, the Canary Island banana is more than a match for its Central American counterpart, but its small size means that it is almost unsaleable on the European market. In addition, it is by no means as competitive. Production on the tiny volcanic island is a lot more labour intensive, and results in much higher costs. In the tropical climate of Costa Rica no irrigation is necessary at all, and wages are also considerably lower. Spain guaranteed a market for the bananas up to the end of 1995, a transitional period of ten years after it joined the EU. After this period, Spain was obliged to admit bananas from other countries. As a result, increasing emphasis has been placed on the development of other products in order to diversify Tenerife's exports, including potatoes, tomatoes, cut flowers and a whole range of exotic fruits.

The largest single source of income for the islanders is now tourism. The number of annual visitors has risen from 30,000 in the late 1950s to 3.5 million. The most significant effects of this rapid rise have been an enlarged job market, increased living costs, settlement of several coastal areas, a steadily increasing (and scarcely satisfied) demand for water because of the immense tourist infrastructure, increased agricultural activity, and last but not least the danger posed to many rare animals and plants.

Environment

Since Spain's entry into the European Union in 1985, the Canary Islands have been gradually forced to adopt the EU's stricter norms. Environmental protection groups are becoming more active and influential and companies as-

The banana boom is over

11

Playa de las Américas

The summer crush

Preserving the natural landscape

sociated with tourism have taken over the responsibility for financing parks and reforestation projects. More important, however, are the political initiatives. Since 1986, the Canary Island parliament has passed a whole series of environmental laws. The autonomous Government's new bills on energy production and use and protection of the coastline in the Canary Archipelago have gone a long way to ensuring that environmental issues feature high on everyone's agenda. The wind park near El Médano (*see page 73*) is just one result of such policies. Meanwhile, moves are still being made to convert more areas of the different islands into national parks. The economic need to diversify in the tourism sector, and respond to past criticism, is leading to positive developments geared towards a 'greener' future for all the islands.

Humboldt on Tenerife

The famous German naturalist and explorer Alexander von Humboldt (1769–1859), after whom the Humboldt Current off the west coast of South America was named, has inspired many a visitor to Tenerife. He spent just one week on Tenerife (and climbed Teide) in June 1799 during a stopover on his way to South and Central America – where he was to spend five years. He never forgot his visit to the island, and in 1814, in his seven-volume *Personal Narrative of Travels to the Equinoctial Regions of the New Continent During the Years 1799 to 1804*, Humboldt wrote the memorable sentence which has been avidly pounced upon since by every tourist manager on Tenerife: 'When one descends into the Valley of Tacoronte, one enters that magnificent land of which travellers from all nations speak with delight. I have seen landscapes in the tropical zone where nature is more magnificent, and the development of organic form has been richer; but having seen the banks of the Orinoco, the Cordillera of Peru and wandered through the beautiful valleys of Mexico, I must confess that I have never been faced by a more varied, attractive scene, with such a harmonious distribution of rock and greenery, anywhere in this world.'

Tenerife's abandoned villages

Most of the abandoned hamlets on the island can be found in the Anaga Las Palmas, for instance, or Las Casillas. They are picturesquely situated, but are not attached to the electricity and water grid. This has made self-sufficiency up here very difficult and local produce has always been hard to sell. The main inducement to leave these villages has simply been the far better wage prospects in the tourist centres. Some farmers still retain their properties just in case they come back some day. Shepherds spend the night in the empty buildings now and then.

Flying the flags

Young people sometimes settle down here, too; first they ask the owner's permission in the neighbouring village, and then move in to their temporary abode, hanging up esoteric artworks. It takes literally hours to go shopping. Not everyone up in these remote places likes visitors, but those who don't mind have plenty of stories to tell about living life close to nature, weird lights in the sky and other such experiences. The local villagers are generally suspicious of the young people as they aren't quite sure what to make of them.

Politics and administration

Since 1982, when the Franco regime in Spain was replaced by a parliamentary democracy with the king as head of state, the Canary Islands have been an autonomous Spanish region with the government seat in Las Palmas on Gran Canaria. The *Cabildo Insular* is the administrative body on each of the islands which is responsible for all decisions above town or village level. It deals, for example, with questions of road construction or environmental protection. Each island is then divided up into municipal districts – Tenerife has 31.

The Canary Islands tend to spring political surprises on a fairly regular basis. After democracy returned, calls for an independent Canary archipelago were at first only voiced by a small left-wing separatist minority. Soon afterwards the moderate right-wing party ATI was formed *(Asociación Tinerfeña Independiente)*, with its demands that the Canaries' special status should be recognised; it was particularly successful in local elections. A recent political development is the *Coalición Canaria*, formed in 1993, a colourful coalition of communists, left-wing and right-wing nationalists and separatists, all of them separate from the PSOE (Spain's ruling social democratic party) and united in their desire to protect 'Canarian interests'.

13

Historical Highlights

c 3000BC Settlement starts on Canary Islands. Finds suggest that the earliest inhabitants were Cro-Magnon people who could have come from the African mainland. They are later followed by at least one more wave of settlers, probably from the Mediterranean area.

From 1200BC Regular visits by Phoenicians and later the Carthaginians. But no trading contacts are established with the original inhabitants, who continue to follow their Stone-Age lifestyle until the Spanish conquest.

c 330BC Aristotle mentions that an island devoid of human habitation off the west coast of Africa was settled by the Carthaginians.

25BC According to an account by Pliny the Elder, King Juba II of Numidia and Mauritania, appointed by Rome, has the Canary Islands explored. Remains of buildings, but no people, are discovered on the eastern islands of Lanzarote and Fuerteventura. Juba II names the type of spurge endemic to Tenerife after his personal physician, Euphorbius.

AD150 The Greek geographer Ptolemy shows the Canary Islands on his map of the world. The map shows the westernmost edge of the known world (his prime meridian) running through the western tip of the island of El Hierro.

1312 The eastern Canary Islands are accidentally rediscovered by a Genoese of Provençal origin named Lanzarote Malocello, when his ship is driven off course on a journey to England. He spends almost 20 years on the island that is later named after him.

1341 Boccaccio mentions four Canarian slaves, goatskins, tallow, red-dyed wood and red earth brought back by the Genoese steersman Niccoloso da Recco. This visit is followed by several plundering expeditions by Genoese, Catalan, Majorcan and Basque seafarers.

1344 Luís de la Cerda, scion of the Spanish House of Castile, is appointed king of the Canary Islands by Pope Clement VI. However, this is only a title and doesn't imply possession. He actually never sets foot on the islands.

1391 Thirteen monks sent to the Canary Islands to spread Christianity are murdered. This is followed by a bloody campaign of revenge against the local population.

1402–6 Robert of Bracamonte, presented with the still-independent Canary Islands by Henry III of Castile, hands them on to his French cousin, Jean de Béthencourt. The latter succeeds in conquering and claiming the islands of Lanzarote, Fuerteventura, El Hierro and later La Gomera on behalf of Spain.

1464 Diego de Herrera and Inés Peraza, the king and queen of Lanzarote, seal a pact with the Guanches in the Bay of Añaza (today's Santa Cruz de Tenerife) which the latter interpret as tantamount to enslavement. The king and queen also build a castle which is promptly destroyed.

1477 Ferdinand of Aragon and Isabella of Castile force Diego de Herrera and Inés Peraza to sell the Canary Islands.

1480 Under the terms of the Treaty of Toledo, Portugal's claim to the Canary Islands is finally abandoned.

1478–83 All remaining Guanche warriors on Gran Canaria are subjugated. One of the Spanish conquerors is Alonso Fernández de Lugo.

1492 After a brief stopover on La Gomera, Christopher Columbus sails on to discover America. During the same year Alonso Fernández de Lugo conquers La Palma.

1494–6 After suffering initial defeat at Matanza de Acentejo, Alonso Fernández de Lugo succeeds after three more campaigns in wresting Tenerife from the Guanches, who have been weakened by a plague epidemic. In the decades that follow, the Canary Islands gradually become an indispensable sea base for trips to America.

1657 An attempt at taking Tenerife is mounted by the English admiral Blake, but it fails.

1706 A renewed attempt by a British fleet to take Tenerife is also unsuccessful. Garachico is destroyed in a volcanic eruption.

1723 Santa Cruz de Tenerife takes over from La Laguna as the capital of the archipelago.

1797 Admiral Nelson suffers the only defeat of his naval career off Santa Cruz, losing his right arm in the process.

1799 Alexander von Humboldt stops over in Tenerife on his way to South America, and climbs Mount Teide.

1817 The first permanent university on the Canary Islands is founded in La Laguna.

1852 Isabella II declares the Canary Islands a free-trade zone.

1890 The British introduce bananas as a monoculture on the archipelago.

1912 Limited self-administration councils (cabildos insulares) are allowed on the islands.

1927 The Canary Islands are divided into two provinces. Santa Cruz de Tenerife becomes capital of the western province, and Las Palmas de Gran Canaria capital of the eastern province.

1936 On July 17 Francisco Bahamonde Franco, the military governor of the Canary Islands, initiates the Spanish Civil War from his residence in Tenerife. Three days later the islands are in the hands of the Fascists.

1978–82 Following the death of Franco and the restoration of the monarchy, the new Spanish constitution joins the two Canary Islands provinces to form the 'Autonomous Region of the Canary Islands'.

1986 Spain joins the European Union and negotiates a special status for the Canary Islands until the end of 1995.

1993 The 'Coalición Canaria', a union of regional parties of the right and left, topples the local parliamentary president. In the national elections on 6 June, the coalition wins four seats and thus becomes the sixth-strongest party in the national parliament in Madrid.

End of 1995 The Canary Islands are fully integrated into the European Union. The islands' free-trade status is in jeopardy.

The Guanches

The mysterious Guanches, the original inhabitants of Tenerife, were considered by their European conquerors to be the fiercest of all the Canary Islanders. They were a Stone Age people, who mummified their dead and buried them in caves. The mummies so far discovered – and also the little written evidence that remains – have led scientists to place the Guanches' ethnic origins in Northwest Africa. Some runes scratched on a stone discovered a few years ago have been transliterated as *zanata*, which is also the name of a Berber tribe, but this may just be speculation.

The earliest European reports are all unanimous about one thing, however – the Guanches had no boats. But it seems strange that there was no contact between Tenerife and nearby La Gomera. And why the Guanches remained firmly in the Stone Age, despite visits from Phoenicians, Romans and Carthaginians, is also a mystery.

Before the Spanish came, Tenerife was divided up into ten different 'princedoms', each run by a so-called *mencey*. All ten shared the summer grazing pastures in Las Cañadas, and were controlled from Adeje by the legendary *Mencey Gran Tinerfe*. The Mencey of Taoro (today's Orotava Valley) occupied a kind of nominal, *primus inter pares* role. The other eight *menceyes* were independent-minded enough to frequently disobey his orders. The tenth administrative district of Tenerife had fallen to a 'poor knight', or *hidalgo*. He was an illegitimate son of the Gran Tinerfe who had been granted his own small dominion. The original Guanche names for these different areas of the island survive even today. These were: Anaga, Güimar, Abona, Adeje, Daute, Icod, Taoro, Tacoronte and Tegueste.

A *mencey* had four main duties, which were to organise agriculture, act as the highest judge and authority, lead his warriors into battle against other *menceyes* or Spanish intruders and communicate with the gods in his capacity as high priest. The most important decisions were made at a raised place of assembly known as a *tagoror*, where the *mencey* sat on a high throne.

Little remains of the Guanches' culture today. They were always too poor. *Gofio*, a flour made from roasted maize, dates back to them, as do special techniques of wrestling and also simple musical instruments. They made their pottery without using wheels; they probably also used the special cultivation method whereby a thin layer of porous pumice is spread across the field so that moisture can be absorbed.

The market in Santa Cruz

Preceding pages:
Playa de las Teresitas

Route 1

★★ Santa Cruz de Tenerife

Santa Cruz de Tenerife (pop. 203,000), the island's capital, is a metropolis with just a trace of provincialism. Its large-town normality is a relief after the sameness of many of the island's tourist centres. Santa Cruz was not built for tourists, and most of its inhabitants work in all kinds of different jobs that have nothing to do with tourism in order to earn their daily bread. The town is not only the joint capital of the archipelago along with Las Palmas on Gran Canaria, it's also the economic, political and social centre of the Canary Islands as a whole.

Santa Cruz began on a small strip of coastline to the south of the Anaga. Today it has spread up the greyish-green surrounding hills and in some places even connects with the outskirts of La Laguna, the island's former capital on the Aguere plain. Rather unattractive, modern residential areas have been built on the edges of Santa Cruz, and it is a credit to the *Tinerfeños* that they have managed to maintain a friendly and sociable atmosphere, with the handful of bars and other meeting places at their disposal here, despite the monotonous bunker-like buildings all around. Santa Cruz has earned the soubriquet *Capital de Amabilidad* (Capital of Friendliness).

Out shopping in Calle de Castillo

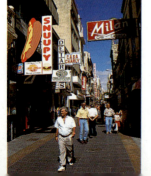

The capital of Tenerife is also the industrial and commercial centre of the island. Industrial zones have sprung up beside these residential areas. One of them, in the south, is a source of continual annoyance because of the eternal flame from its oil refinery and the pollution it causes. The harbour has become a lot quieter ever since the worldwide shipbuilding recession, but business life continues unabated on the Castillo (the main street in Santa Cruz)

and its surrounding streets. In fact competition has, if anything, become tougher over the past years. Street traders are now forbidden to sell their wares here.

The centre of Santa Cruz de Tenerife is an attractive mixture of the older quarters, which still contain the odd art nouveau jewel, modern architecture, which isn't always that pleasing to the eye, and blossom-filled boulevards, ramblas, parks and squares.

Cultural life is very varied indeed, and ranges from the magnificent symphony concerts in the Teatro Guimerá to the much-promoted beauty contests in the KU disco, and from ear-splitting rock concerts in the Plaza de Toros to the week-long, procession-filled religious worship of the Madonna of Light from Candelaria.

A mixture of styles

History

The strip of coastline on which Santa Cruz de Tenerife lies was originally the bridgehead of the Spanish *Conquista*. Alonso de Lugo built a fort on the beach in 1494 and used it as a base for his sorties inland. Two years later, when the Guanches had been completely subjugated, he founded the town of Santa Cruz here. It developed into a trading base for the three-way intercontinental trade between Europe, Africa and America, gradually taking over from Tenerife's other harbours of Garachico and Puerto de la Cruz. In 1723 it was made capital of the island in place of La Laguna, and nearly 100 years later it became the capital of the entire archipelago.

Santa Cruz had already been accorded the royal privilege of trading with America in 1778, bringing in even more income for its merchants. Three British attempts to capture the strategically important town were repulsed. In 1797, during the last British attack, Admiral Nelson lost not only the battle but his right arm as well. Three lion's heads in the municipal coat of arms stand as a reminder of this skirmish, and there's also a public holiday in August to celebrate the victory. From then on the town was left in peace by everyone apart from the Spanish.

In 1927 the Canary Islands were divided up into two provinces, and Santa Cruz became the capital of the western one, made up of Tenerife, La Palma, La Gomera and El Hierro. With the demise of the Franco regime in 1982 this division also came to an end, and the archipelago was made into an autonomous community (*comunidad autónoma*) under the joint administration of Santa Cruz de Tenerife and Las Palmas on Gran Canaria. Both towns had been competing to become the capital of the whole group and the rivalry between them has not been laid to rest to this day. Now the presidency changes towns every four years, while the parliament resides permanently in Santa Cruz.

Monumento de los Caídos and Palacio Insular

Sights

The most important sights in Santa Cruz de Tenerife can be divided up into two strolls, neither of which is too demanding, plus a brief extra section. The starting point for both walks is the Plaza de España, firstly because it's easily reached from outside Santa Cruz, secondly because there are supervised car parks there, and thirdly because the adjacent Plaza de la Candelaria lies at the very heart of the town.

Walk 1: from the old to the new

The old centre of Santa Cruz is bordered by the Rambla del General Franco and the streets that join it to the west. In the middle of the Plaza de España stands the **Monumento de los Caídos ❶**, erected in honour of those who fought for Franco in the Spanish Civil War (1936–39). The centre of the monument has been designed as an observation tower in the form of a high cross with shortened sides, and the plinth contains a small remembrance chapel. The tower has been closed ever since it became a May Day target for Canarian separatists during the 1970s, so unfortunately cannot be climbed.

On the south side of the square facing the sea is the ★ **Palacio Insular ❷**, with the striking clock tower on its

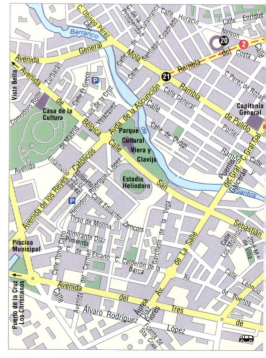

corner. This public building is where the island council (*Cabildo Insular*) meets, and the **municipal tourist office** (*Oficina de turismo*) is housed on its ground floor. A glass window near the entrance to the Palacio Insular shows the Tenerife coat of arms, surrounded by plants typical of the island. The conference hall (*salón de actos*) is usually closed to the public but its walls feature mythical depictions by José Ahuiar, painted in the Mexican muralist style. A glockenspiel in the clock tower plays a Canarian folk tune named *Tajaraste*, after a traditional tambourine-like instrument. The ★★ **Archaeological Museum** (*Museo Arqueologico de Tenerife*, Tuesday to Saturday 10am–5pm, Sunday 10am–2pm) which used to be housed inside this building is now in the process of being moved a few streets further away to the **Antiguo Hospital Civil** ❹, a former hospital on the other side of the Barranco de Santos. A small exhibition entitled *Los Guanches* can already be enjoyed at the museum's new location.

The Main Post Office

The other monumental structure on the Plaza de España is the **Main Post Office**.

Take the Avenida de Bravo Murillo now, which leads between the post office and the Palacio Insular. This street and the Avenida de José Antonio Primo di Rivera on the seaward side both constitute Santa Cruz's 'main drag'.

21

**ROUTE 1
SANTA CRUZ
DE TENERIFE**

0   300m

Iglesia Nostra Señora de la Concepción

Follow the Avenida de Bravo Murillo as far as the oldest church in town, the ★★ **Iglesia Nostra Señora de la Concepción ❸**. Built in 1502, it was destroyed in a fire exactly 150 years later. It was rebuilt in the baroque style, and the architecture is quite simple on the outside. The octagonal tower served as a lookout post. The unplastered corners of the walls are a typical decorative feature of buildings in the Canary Islands. The church's entrance portico is surrounded by balconies, and the low-ceilinged, five-aisled interior culminates in the magnificently decorated high altar at the end of the central nave. Note the richly painted ceiling and also the finely carved choirstalls.

In the **Chapel of the Holy Heart** is the cross from which the town derives its name: it was placed in the sand of Añaza Beach by the island's conqueror, Alonso de Lugo, when he claimed the island for Spain. Añaza was the Guanche name for the area occupied by Santa Cruz today. The floor of the chapel next door, dedicated to St James, contains the tomb of General Gutierez, the man who successfully defeated Lord Nelson, and buried beside him is the classical composer Teobaldo Power.

The ★★ **Natural History Museum** (Tuesday to Saturday 10am–5pm, Sunday 10am–2pm) is also being housed in the old hospital mentioned above ❹. This has got off to a good start with an exhibition called *Sea and Coasts of the Canaries* (*Mar y Costas de Canarias*).

Walk up the avenue of San Sebastián now to reach the ★ **Mercado de Nuestra Señora de Africa ❺**. This central market is a food emporium piled high with fresh produce, revealing just how bountiful Mother Nature is here on Tenerife. A very hectic place, and not for late risers, it's more akin to an Oriental bazaar than anything else. The surrounding cafés are no less tumultuous, and not the place for a tranquil snack. On Sundays, it hosts a flea market that draws quite a few locals from round about. Handmade jewellery, mass-produced junk and exotic imports all lie out in the bright Canarian sunshine waiting for buyers. Beer and *café con leche* are served in the market cafés.

Fresh blooms in the market

Take the General Serrador Bridge and head back towards the centre. The rather unassuming-looking building on the right hand side of the Imeldo Seris is the **Teatro Guimerá ❻**. This municipal theatre was named after the playwright Angel Guimerá (1849–1924), who was born in Santa Cruz. While still a boy he moved with his parents to Catalonia, and in Barcelona became a famous Catalan poet and dramatist. His best known play is *Terra Baixa* (1896), on which Eugen d'Albert based his opera *Tiefland* (1903). The theatre does not have a full-time acting troupe, which means that it is only used sporadically for major concerts and minor theatre, cabaret and ballet performances.

Teatro Guimerá

The Museo Municipal

A former market hall next to the theatre functions as a gallery for photographic and art exhibitions, the **Centro de Fotografía** ❼ (Tuesday to Saturday 10am–1pm and 5–8pm, Sunday 11am–1pm).

Cross the Imeldo Seris next, and follow the Valentín Sanz as far as the ★★ **Parque del Príncipe de Asturias** ❽. The small park lies in the shade of several enormous Indian laurel trees, and the pavilion in the centre is often used for concerts. The restaurant nearby resembling an art nouveau greenhouse is a good place for a meal, or just a coffee break. Those keen on modern architecture should walk a short distance northwestwards at this point, to the enormous ★ **Canary Bank Building** ❾. It was built in 1987 and is the combined work of three local architects, Artengo, Domínguez and Schwartz. Its mirror exterior is mainly composed of brown-tinted glass. On the northeastern side of the Parque del Príncipe is the newly renovated facade of the **Círculo de Amistad XII de Enero**, a well-known cultural centre.

The ★★★ **Museo Municipal** ❿ (Monday to Friday 10am–1.45pm and 2.30–6.45pm in summer, Monday to Friday 10am–8pm in winter, admission free) at the other end of the park is definitely worth a visit. It contains numerous collections of sculpture and ceramic art by Canarian artists and painters (de Guezala, Bonnín, Aguiar, de la Torre), and also several Spanish and Dutch old masters including works by de Rivera, de Miranda, van Loo and Jordaens. The facade of the building is adorned with busts of famous Canarian poets, philosophers and musicians. The municipal library is also housed here.

Beyond the museum, in the same complex of buildings, is the baroque **Church of San Francisco** ⓫. Founded in 1680, this building originally belonged to a convent which used to own the Parque del Príncipe and other land

The Church of San Francisco

nearby. The church has excellent acoustics and is regularly used for organ concerts. Also noteworthy are the 17th and 18th-century retables (shelves or frames enclosing decorated panels behind altars), the frescoed ceiling and several 18th-century paintings.

Walk downhill now as far as the Alameda del Duque de Santa Elena, which used to be the town's main *paseo* (the part of town where strolling, flirting, chatting, seeing and being seen takes place after siesta time, *see page 78*). The British bar on the corner of the Plaza de Candelaria is a good place to wind up this brief tour. Take a seat, watch the passers-by and relax.

Walk 2: dignified squares and beautiful views

Discussing events on Plaza de la Candelaria

The **Plaza de la Candelaria** ⓬ is named after the statue (at the lower end) depicting a Madonna and child. It is meant to portray the victory of Christianity over the subjugated 'pagan' Guanches, four of whom can be seen standing at the foot of the obelisk. This statue has often wrongly been attributed to the sculptor Canova, as it was probably executed by the Genoese artist Pasquale Bocciardo in 1773, shortly after he provided the cathedral in La Laguna with its marble pulpit.

The building at the northern corner of the square houses the Casino de Tenerife, which is no gambling den but an elegant private club. Only the authorised may enter. The interior is exceptionally magnificent and colourful and was decorated by such famous Canarian artists as de Guezala, Bonnín, de la Torre and Aguiar.

A little further up on the same side of the square is the **Palacio de los Rodríquez Carta**, with its dark-grey basalt facade. This former patrician's house dating from 1742 is now occupied by a bank. The banking hall is situated

The Castillo, a pedestrian precinct

in the patio, which is surrounded by balconies of dark, polished Canary pine. The patio can be admired in the mornings, during normal business hours.

At its upper end, the square merges into the town's main shopping street, the **Castillo**, which is a pedestrian precinct. The Castillo and the side streets nearby are filled with one boutique and department store after another. You will also find a number of shops owned by Indians, offering cut-price electronic articles, cameras, cheap perfumes and souvenirs. Don't worry about haggling here – it's an accepted practice! The street cafés with their sunshades provide plenty of welcome relief from the hectic bargain-hunting. The section of town a bit further uphill to the right contains a number of clothes shops and is considerably more expensive.

The side street named after Teobaldo Power contains the **Parlamento de Canarias** ⓭, set back slightly with its neoclassical portico, the permanent home of the Canarian parliament.

At the fork between the Castillo and the Robayna stands the ★★ **Casa Elder** ⓮, a very fine art nouveau relic with a striking carved wooden door. Its architect, Antonio Pintor, was active around the turn of the century and designed several large-scale projects on the island including the Town Hall and bullfighting arena in Santa Cruz, and also the Teatro Leal in La Laguna. The Casa Elder houses a good bookshop called La Isla, which stocks a great deal of local literature on the Canary Islands.

Plaza de Weyler

The **Plaza de Weyler** cannot be described as an oasis of tranquillity – it's simply too small for that. But the middle of it is still quite charming, with its marble *Fuente del Amor* (Fountain of Love), the work of Genoese sculptor Achille Caresse. The building that overlooks the square is altogether less delightful – it's the **Capitanía General**, the island's military headquarters. General Franco was in charge here briefly just before the outbreak of the Spanish Civil War.

Stained glass, Gobierno Civil

Follow the Méndez Núñez down to the right now, and on the left the main municipal administration building, the **Gobierno Civil** ⓯, comes into view. It's not usually open to visitors, but the walls of its conference chamber give a pictorial representation of Canarian history and also several idyllic local scenes showing *Tinerfeños* in folk dress.

Town Hall door detail

The building just next door on the corner is the **Ayuntamiento** ⓰ (Town Hall), designed by Antonio Pintor in 1898. The town's coat of arms is visible above the entrance in the Viera y Clavijo. The statues in the portico emphasise the building's neoclassical style, which is punctuated by the odd art nouveau element. The rich and ornate conference chamber is usually only seen by mem-

A surviving frog
A bench of tiles

FABRICA DE SALAZONES
PLAYA DE SANTIAGO
• GOMERA •

bers of the civic council, but its ceiling features an allegorical fresco by González Méndez depicting *The Victory of Truth over Ignorance*. Two glass domes add extra light to the room. There are several other illustrations with scientific and artistic themes and a portrait of the monarch hangs high on the wall.

Further up the hill there's an inviting little round square called the ★ **Plaza 25 de Julio** ⑰ with a fountain made of *azulejos* (tiles) from Seville. At the edge of the fountain there were once a total of eight glazed frogs spouting water, competing with the colourful bird at the centre. The frogs tended to get kissed rather roughly, however, and instead of turning into princes they shattered into fragments, much to the dismay of the town council. The tiled benches are also attractive.

The area surrounding this square, and the side streets across to the west on the other side of the Rambla, contain the finest collection of turn-of-the-century villas in Santa Cruz. One particularly fine example is the ★ **Casa Quintero** ⑱. Its elegant stucco foliate forms an exciting contrast to the lush vegetation in the front garden.

A pedestrian avenue between two streets leads directly to the western end of the town's finest park. The **Parque Municipal García Sanabria** ⑲ was named after one of the town's mayors and covers a full 6ha (15 acres) of land. It has long and leafy pedestrian avenues, sparkling fountains and mosaic benches shaded by bamboo. Modern sculpture, which has been an additional feature of the park since the 1970s, contrasts well with the luxuriant vegetation. The number of different varieties of plants here is quite astonishing. The café next to a floral clock with a glockenspiel and large red hands provides delicious Spanish snacks known as *tapas*, along with cake, ice cream and other refreshments.

Variety in the Parque Municipal

When the *paseo* (*see page 78*) begins towards late afternoon, cross from the park to the Rambla General Franco and continue in a westerly direction towards the Plaza de la Paz. On the way there is a former bullfighting **arena** ⑳ which is mainly used for open-air pop concerts nowadays. This whole area of the town can't avoid the din, of course, so those with broad tastes in music are lucky. On the **Plaza de la Paz** ㉑ itself, there's an old-fashioned, plush Cine Victor cinema which often shows Hollywood films with Spanish subtitles.

There's an extremely good view of Santa Cruz and its harbour to be had from an observation point (*mirador*) up on the winding road to La Laguna via La Cuesta. It's marked as a photo spot and is called **Vista Bella**.

Route 2

★★ Puerto de la Cruz

Since the 1960s, Puerto de la Cruz (pop. 40,000) has developed from a small fishing village into the largest tourist centre on the north coast. Although Playa de las Américas in the south overtook it in popularity quite some while ago, Puerto de la Cruz still has quite a few positive aspects. However, it should be mentioned that the weather in the north of the island certainly is rather cooler than in the south, and that the sun can often be hidden by a veil of grey cloud for days at a time. It certainly isn't cold, though – not even at night.

A place to meet the locals

Nevertheless, Puerto de la Cruz possesses something Las Américas can only dream of and that's a traditional town centre which serves as a popular meeting place for locals and tourists alike. Despite all the unattractive box-like hotels, a lot of the old town centre remains, which provides quite a bit of original flair. Even the beaches here have their own special attractions – the new Playa Jardín with its dark, volcanic sand is as much a joy to the eye as the famous Lago Martiánez sea-water swimming pool. Hikers will find an almost endless range of possibilities in the area above Orotava, and the temperatures are just right – not too hot, not too cold.

27

History

After the *Conquista*, Puerto de la Cruz was the harbour for merchants from Villa Orotava, and at that time was known as Puerto de Orotava. It was officially recognised as a harbour by the Spanish crown in 1603. The fishing harbour, protected on both sides by a jetty, is all that remains today of the three former moorings. The freight that ar-

The old harbour

rived here was either transferred to the main harbours at Garachico or Santa Cruz on small ships to be unloaded there, or taken out in small boats to larger ships at anchor further out. The fort of San Felipe, still in existence today, and the coastal batteries at San Telmo and Santa Barbara – both of them now little more than ruins – were originally meant to protect the trading vessels anchored here from enemy attack.

When Garachico was destroyed by a volcanic eruption in 1706, Puerto de la Cruz immediately grew in importance as the only harbour on the north coast. It dissociated itself from Orotava and became an independent commune. However, the collapse of the wine trade in the late 19th century combined with road improvements all over the island, finally sounded the death knell for the harbour, which had always been fairly inaccessible anyway. The new capital of Santa Cruz gradually attracted all the overseas trade.

At the end of the 19th century, rich English visitors were discovering Puerto de la Cruz and beginning to spend their winters in the spring climate here. By the turn of the century, the idyllic fishing village had become a popular spa resort, and today's Casino Taoro is the original sanatorium. It wasn't until after World War II that tourism finally began to grow in Puerto. Despite the odd crisis, investment in tourism continues here, and construction work is still going on.

The Playa Jardín

Sights

Those arriving by car from outside the town should take the easternmost exit to Puerto de la Cruz and then follow signs to the centre, passing the Botanical Gardens (*Jardín Botánico*) on the way. The observation point on the right, signposted as Mirador de la Paz, provides a good view of the whole town. Cars may be parked here, then it's just a short way down the steps to the **Centro Comercial Martiánez ❶**. Or if you like, drive on a bit further and use the car park at the new shopping centre.

Begin this stroll along the seafront by following the pedestrian avenue that leads down from the Centro Martiánez to the Playa of the same name, where surfers can often be seen showing off their talents. The town's administration is planning to give the present bathing area a facelift. There are free bus rides and also a miniature railway from here to the Parrot Park (*Loro Parque*).

The left-hand side of the Avenida de Colón is lined with one café after another, all of them with roadside terraces. Stretching away to the right are the ★★ **Lago Martiánez** and the ★★ **Lido de San Telmo ❷**, both designed by the brilliant Lanzarote artist César Manrique, who died tragically in 1992 (*see page 76*). This complex was built in 1977, and Manrique's exclusive use of local materials creates an organic composition. Menhir-like stones smoothed by sea water, tree stumps bleached by the sun,

Lago Martiánez

29

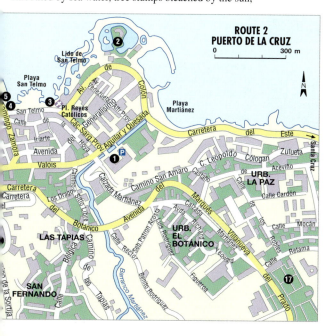

The San Telmo chapel

The Town Hall

Casa de la Real Aduana

palisades, playful sculpture, and red-and-white fantastic creatures form a highly impressive ensemble that has earned much public acclaim.

The underground nightclub, Andromeda, on the Isla del Lago presents a topless, Moulin Rouge-style show in the evenings, while elsewhere on the complex there's 'live' Latin-American music providing plenty of opportunity for dancing. Portrait artists and caricaturists work long into the tropical evening round here.

The 'pedestrian precinct proper' begins at the simple white chapel of ★ **San Telmo** ❸. This picturesque little building was built on the site of a coastal battery in 1780, and is consecrated to the patron saint of mariners. Church services are held here regularly in a variety of different languages including English and German. A bit further along the promenade the sea can get rather choppy, and almost seems to be boiling whenever there's a storm. The spray flies up over the embankment and on to the promenade, with its noisy row of amusement arcades. At the end of it, steps lead up to the **Punta del Vento** ❹, where the trade winds usually blow straight into your face off the sea. The rather unappealing, wind-battered sculpture here by local artist Arnoldo Evora is called *Spectator*.

Stay close to the sea and follow the Santo Domingo down to the right. The first building on the right once formed part of the Dominican monastery of **San Pedro González Telmo** ❺, built in 1659. Partially destroyed by fire in 1778, it finally fell victim to state secularisation in 1837 and is now privately owned.

Next door is the **Town Hall** ❻, and beyond it is the generously proportioned **Plaza de Europa**, which is highly reminiscent of an old coastal fortress with its battlements and ancient cannon. A car park has been built beneath it. Despite the fountain and the odd bench, the square appears rather sterile and lacking in greenery.

Head towards the harbour now, where things start to cheer up again. Even though the number of fishing boats here has declined in recent years, several do still operate and give the place a suitably romantic atmosphere, with plenty of sights and smells. The small alley called Las Lonjas is distinctly fishy. The harbour also boasts the oldest secular structure in town, the **Casa de la Real Aduana** ❼. This ancient building became the customs house and residence of the royal tax collector after Garachico was destroyed in the volcanic eruption of 1706. In 1833, Santa Cruz took over tax administration instead, and since then the building has been privately owned. Local families can often be observed in the harbour here at weekends, having picnics on the pebble beach.

Beyond the harbour there is a vast expanse of waste ground, the site of the municipal administration's most ambitious plan. Expensive land reclamation has provided the town with an extra 100,000sq m (119,600sq yards) of ground to build a sea park (*Parque Marítimo Municipal*). The architect-artist César Manrique contributed to the project shortly before his death. Many attractions are planned, including a Disneyland-style entertainment centre, a fun park and pool, mini-golf, artificial lakes, cultural centres, restaurants, shopping streets and restful parks.

From the harbour a broad street leads to the main square and focus of the town's social life **Plaza del Charco** ❽. Resembling a raised podium, and shaded by 150-year-old laurels, this square is a forum, a stage and an auditorium rolled into one. It's the place to meet friends, drink your *café cortado* (*see Food & Drink, page 81*) on the terrace of the popular Dinámico café, buy an English newspaper from the nearby kiosk and soak up the southern sunshine. Concerts are sometimes held here, and so are wine-tastings. Some of the buildings on the western side of the square (mostly restaurants) have retained their attractive Canarian appearance.

Enjoy a terrace view…

31

Leave the square at its northwestern corner and head for the still partly preserved fishermen's quarter known as La Ranilla, with its narrow streets and tiny houses. The food served in the tiny restaurants here is really quite good, and there's a pleasant, 'family-run' atmosphere about the whole place. In the middle of the *Barrio* there's an **Archaeological Museum** ❾ (Tuesday to Saturday 10am–1pm and 5–9pm, Sunday 10am–1pm) inside a 19th-century Canarian town house. It contains several relics from the Guanche period, including ceramics and mum-

…or the local atmosphere

Fun at San Felipe fort
Black sand at Playa Jardín

Resident of the Parrot Park

Inside San Francisco

mified remains, and also fascinating collections of old maps, weapons and butterflies.

On the other side of La Ranilla there are several modern buildings, but then a football pitch and a swimming pool come into view. Just beyond them is the little 17th-century fort of **San Felipe** ❿. Cannon in the square outside it stand as reminders of its former function. It was a restaurant until a short time ago, and is now due to become a cultural centre for exhibitions and concerts.

Next comes the long expanse of the ★ **Playa Jardín** ⓫, with its broad, curving bays. César Manrique had a hand in the design here, too. Black, volcanic sand was excavated from the sea and then kept from being washed back by breakwaters. To the rear of the beach a park has been laid out containing typical Canarian flora, an old winepress, an artificial waterfall, a music pavilion, changing rooms, showers, restaurants, bars and footpaths – all of it hugely popular. The shiny, black rock amidst the crashing surf, and the steep cliffs in the distance give the Playa Jardín its unmistakeably individual attraction. This stretch of coast doesn't even pretend to be a South Seas paradise – and that's what makes it quite unique.

In Punta Brava at the end of the Playa Jardín is the much-praised ★★ **Parrot Park** ⓬, which contains the largest single collection of parrots in any park in the world. Of the 300 or so species here, several are facing extinction and it's one of the aims of the park to rescue them. There are also tigers, gorillas, chimpanzees, crocodiles, flamingoes, bats, sea lions, sharks and dolphins plus a varied collection of plants, including an extensive orchid garden. Parrot, sea-lion and dolphin shows are put on regularly and an African market and Thai village make the whole place even more exotic.

From the Parrot Park it's possible to get back to where you started by miniature railway. Another option would be to take the train as far as Plaza del Charco and then walk back to the Quintana pedestrian precinct and over to the sea promenade. A few flights of steps here lead up to a small square with a group of well-tended buildings. Opposite, on the left, are the ★★ **Hermitage of San Juan** and the ★★ **Church of San Francisco** ⓭, both of which are definitely worth a visit. Evening time is best, when the interiors and the retables (shelves or frames enclosing decorated panels behind altars) are at their most magnificent. After San Amaro in the La Paz section of town, the hermitage is the oldest building in Puerto de la Cruz. It was consecrated to St John the Baptist in around 1600. The area formerly occupied by the Franciscan monastery is today known as the Parque de San Francisco, and contains a building devoted to cultural events, ranging from children's ballet and folklore to classical tragedy.

Make a short detour southwards along the San Juan, past a cinema and at the junction with the Triarte is a well-preserved 18th-century building, the ★ **Casa Triarte** , birthplace of Tenerife's best-known storyteller Don Tomás de Triarte (1755–91). Today the building is used for commercial purposes. The lone tower nearby used to belong to the Palacio Ventoso and is the last of its kind. In the old days every commercial building had such a tower from which trading vessels could be espied from afar, thus allowing the owner of the house to reach the harbour and negotiate with the captain before anyone else.

The town's parish church, the ★★ **Iglesia Nuestra Señora de la Peña de Francia** , stands on a raised square on the Quintana. It contains one of the most emotive Madonna statues in Spain, by José Luján Pérez from Gran Canaria. The statue of Santo Domingo is probably by him as well. Four of the paintings on the evangelist side of the retable and five panels on the pulpit are by a local painter, Luis de la Cruz. The statue of St Peter is the work of Fernando Estévez from Orotava. The church also contains some fine Canarian and Cuban gold and silverwork.

Iglesia Nuestra Señora de la Peña de Francia

The **tourist information office** is on the square outside the church. At the end of the Quintana is the sea promenade, which leads back to the starting point of the tour.

33

Excursions

Above the town centre, surrounded by a delightfully restful park, is the 100-year-old **Casino Taoro** (daily 7pm–3am, Friday and Saturday until 4am). Those eager to help fill the coffers of the Spanish state should bring along their passport and lots of money. Men are no longer requested to wear a tie. The Hotel Tigaiga is also in the park. For tourists, every Sunday, it has hosted an introduction to the mysteries of *lucha Canaria*, the specialised form of wrestling that dates back to the days of the Guanches (*see page 15*). The proceedings are rounded off with dancing and folk music.

The Casino Taoro park

The world-famous ★★★ **Jardín Botánico** (daily 9am–6pm), above the La Paz section of town, provides a fascinating glimpse of the island's flora and also contains exotic species from all of the Spanish colonies. It was first started as an acclimatisation garden in 1788, where tropical plants were gradually accustomed to the far cooler climate of the royal residences of Central Spain. The experiment proved unsuccessful, but the Botanical Gardens remained – not least because of the effort put in by Swiss gardener and biologist Hermann Josef Wildpret, who took over the neglected site in 1860. Even though more than 3,000 exotic plants here are labelled in three languages (Latin, English and Spanish), it's still worth bringing along a good tropical plant guidebook.

Route 3

The bizarre landscape of the Teno Mountains

Playa de las Américas – Adele – Barranco del Infierno – Masca – Buenavista – Punta del Teno – Los Silos – Erjos Pass – Los Gigantes (123km/76 miles)

This is a trip back through time which leaves hyper-modernity behind and leads into the last refuges of a rural life close to the land in the Teno Mountains. There's no South Seas flora kept alive by artificial irrigation round here, but bizarre natural rock formations that have taken several million years to evolve.

Bar by the beach

The starting point of this route is the resort of ★ **Playa de las Américas**, a modern-day Garden of Eden, in which the island's inhospitable volcanic landscape can be completely ignored. Many people regard the twin agglomerations of Los Cristianos and Las Américas, bravely sited and entirely dependent on artificial waterways, as a horrific vision of things to come in the 21st century. The Mediterranean-style apartments are all jammed closely together, and stretch up the dusty mountain slopes close to the coast.

The various expensive hotels near the beach can best be viewed from up in the mountains, along with all the other architecture, some of it dreadful, some a little more imaginative. The latter includes several pompous classical, neo-Canarian and postmodern structures, some of them in cool marble, others made of glass and steel – there's hardly an architectural style that hasn't been exploited.

At first sight, Las Américas is definitely grandiose with its enormous buildings, the masses of people crowding the promenades, and the busy traffic. But this glitzy world was built on top of one country estate (*finca*) and a handful of banana plantations, and lacks a proper town centre. Instead, there's a long strip of beach extending from Los Cristianos to Fañabé, with several busy shops along it. Note all the warning signs: this place is a paradise for pick-pockets and confidence tricksters.

Tranquillity can be found

Take an evening stroll here and you'll also be deaf-ened by music from every European country being played simultaneously, some of it even accompanied by the live singing of *karaoke* performers. The worst place is prob-ably the Las Verónicas nightclub near the Barranco del Rey, where mainly British youths dance and perspire away on three levels, and Lolita-like young women entice cus-tomers into the techno din with promises of 'Happy Hour' and/or a 'free drink'. A significantly large number of uniformed officials do their utmost to main-tain a semblance of order.

People looking for peace and quiet retreat to ho-tel swimming pool areas, which are usually stud-ded with suitably attractive flora. Although there are weekly entertainment programmes here, they're usually reasonably quiet and harmless. It's only in the hotels which have their own discos that participation sometimes gets a bit out of hand.

Anyone looking for sections of empty beaches will usually be disappointed, especially in peak season – there again, all year round seems to be peak season here! Those seeking picturesque beaches will be forced to realise that there's still quite a bit of construction work going on, and that the various palm trees that have been planted will need another few decades to reach a respectable height and provide much-needed shade.

All in all, apart from its sunny climate, fertile volcanic soil and eagerness to cater for tourists, Las Américas has very little in common with the rest of Tenerife. It's an enclave of international tourism, and functions according to the same mar-keting principles. It's impossible to ignore the way in which the locals jostle each other to extract money from the masses of visitors here – not ex-actly the ideal atmosphere for a holiday. There again, those after sunshine, a full swimming pool or beach, sports activities and lots of noisy evening activities all within a few yards of each other have definitely come to the right place. Visitors from all over the world continue to contribute to the tourist boom here, so it's hard to sympathise with the lo-cal promoters' complaints that business is not do-ing as well as it could be.

Leave Las Américas on the southern motorway, which has now been completed and extends as far as Torviscas. It then turns into a narrower, but still well-surfaced country road with several bends. To the right is the **Conde** (1,003m/3,290ft), the most striking-looking mountain in the south of Tenerife; its slopes are covered with flowers in the springtime. If the thermals are good, hang-gliders can often be seen descending to the coast from the top (*see page 86*).

★ **Adeje**, a small village steeped in history, has profited from its role as administration centre for Las Américas, and has spread from its original site up on the slopes of the famous ravine, the Barranco del Infierno, almost as far as the valley road. The long Generalisimo Franco, the main street, climbs steadily upwards and is lined by houses which have successfully retained their original villagey appearance. Most people visit Adeje to walk along the Barranco del Infierno (*see page 37*).

Life at a more sedate pace

A church at the upper end of the laurel-shaded street, the **Iglesia Santa Ursula**, still bears traces of the village's feudal origins. The Condes de la Gomera, Marqueses de Adeje and Señores de Hierro who were in power at the time could attend services by peering through a barred balcony above the sacristy.

Their manor house, the **Casa Fuerte**, is still partially preserved. It was from here during the 16th century that the Pontes, a Genoese merchant family, carried on a profitable illegal trade with Latin America – partly with the assistance of the pirate John Hawkins. The merchandise included English cloth, home-made sugar and African slaves. The Pontes owned horses in Andalusia and also a herd of camels. The Casa Fuerte is not what it once was, but to reach it turn left at the church, opposite the right

The Casa Fuerte

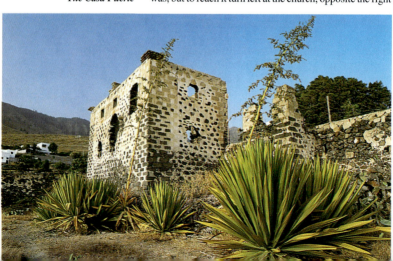

turn leading up to the Barranco del Infierno. An old cannon stands in the square outside the building, which is privately owned.

The ★★ **Barranco del Infierno** provides a particularly good foretaste of what Tenerife has to offer hikers. A *barranco* is a gorge on the slopes of a volcano which probably formed when the ground tore open during the original eruption, and later became so deep when its base was eroded. It should be added that the two steep sides of the Barranco del Infierno actually belong to two different mountain ranges: the older Adeje massif and the younger Teide range. In the past, numerous mummies of the island's original inhabitants, the Guanches, have been discovered in caves in the southeastern wall.

Exploring the Barranco del Infierno

The round walk takes roughly three hours in all, the path is clearly marked and there are hardly any steep bits. It's best to wear sturdy shoes, because it's no promenade either. In the style of the late César Manrique, the Canary Islands' most famous artist, the steeper sections of the footpath have been strengthened and lined with wooden palisades. Halfway along the walk there's a small rivulet with some fascinating reed formations along its banks. The hike ends at a waterfall, whose three cascades fall into a small gravelled basin, which can be very spectacular depending on the time of year. This is a good place to stop for a snack. After the hike, how about an introduction to the delights of Canarian cuisine? At the entrance to the *barranco* there's a charming little restaurant with a view (*see page 81*).

The road along the mountain slope now leads through some *malpaís* ('badlands'). Despite the inhospitable terrain, the rock's high water content has turned **Guía de Isora** into a small agricultural centre, growing mainly tomatoes and potatoes. The church in this quiet little village contains two Madonnas by José Luján Pérez, Tenerife's most famous baroque woodcarver. Down on the coast at the Playa de San Juan, tourism is already starting to make its mark. In the harbour, protected by its large jetty, there's a pebble beach that takes some getting used to.

The direct route to Santiago del Teide leads up to **Arguayo**, a village that has rediscovered hand-made pottery, and even has a museum, **Centro Alfarero**, devoted to ceramics (Monday to Saturday 10am–1pm and 4–7pm). The road winds its way onward through the foothills of the island's most recent lava field (the eruption here took place in 1909). On the other side of a mountain ridge, ★ **Santiago del Teide** suddenly comes into view, situated very picturesquely in a high valley. There's not a lot to see in this little village apart from its whitewashed church, scarcely a century old, and a couple of disused winepresses (*lagar*).

Santiago del Teide

37

Masca is a real gem

The narrow road to Masca

The real attraction here is the location, with its unobstructed view of Teide (3,717m/12,194ft).

At the top of the pass leading to ★★★ **Masca**, the gem of the Teno region, the view of Teide is particularly impressive. In the opposite direction, the island of La Palma can be seen in the distance. If the visibility's good, La Gomera looks almost close enough to touch even though it's actually 30km (18 miles) away. The road gets very narrow on its way down to Masca, and there are several sharp bends. Until the mid-1970s this village was only accessible from Santiago and El Palmar along a footpath and an old mule track. Today at least a dozen tourist buses arrive here daily, not to mention the numerous jeeps and rental cars. It's no wonder, really, considering the wild mountain scenery and the various idyllically located bars and restaurants.

The real highlight of Masca for experienced hikers is the descent into the ★★★ **Barranco de Masca**. It takes around two hours. The return trip takes almost double that time. Bring sturdy shoes, sun protection including a hat, and enough drinking water too, because the heat tends to get trapped inside the island's gorges. The bizarre, volcanic mountain scenery with its strange flora is unforgettable. There's the odd rivulet with reeds and red dragonflies, and the bleating of goats can often be heard as they graze higher up. Camping out overnight in gorges is forbidden for environmental reasons, but it's extremely dangerous anyway because *barrancos* tend to echo regularly with the sound of falling rocks.

A popular way to get to the gorge is by boat, and some people hire the services of local fishermen from Los Gigantes, thus saving themselves the descent. The sea can get quite choppy, though, and if you go swimming take care, as there are several rocks hidden just below the water and the undertow can be dangerous.

Beyond Masca the road becomes even more narrow and bendy, so it's a good idea to sound your horn regularly. Up on the pass, a powerful trade wind often blows great ragged pieces of cloud across the ridge. At the very top, the high valley of **El Palmar** comes into view. It is dominated by a volcanic cone which looks as if it has been eroded in several places, but, in fact, it is just where the fertile ash has been quarried for the banana plantations. The air up here is filled with the aroma of wild fennel and other herbs.

In El Palmar itself a small asphalt road leads off to the small village of ★ **Teno Alto**. Time really seems to have stopped here. A few solitary houses stand in the middle of the high plain. Anything that's not in regular use in the bar is simply left to gather dust. A cold wind blows across the plateau, making the whole region seem even more inhospitable. In some places the earth is coloured red due to iron oxide. Most of the local inhabitants here are goatherds, and only a generation ago most of them still knew how to swing themselves across from one side of a *barranco* to the other using their crooks.

A local goatherd

39

The peaceful village of ★ **Buenavista** lies on the northern coast just round from the Punta del Teno (*see below*). Its village square contains one of the little pavilions so typical of the island, and is a good place to stop for a coffee. Visit the **church of Nuestra Señora de los Remedios** and admire its fascinating Mudéjar-style ceiling. The statue of St Francis, thought to be the work of Spanish sculptor Alonso Cano, is also striking.

Feel like an unusual bathing experience? Then head for the gravel beach known as the **Playa de los Barcos**, where the small, narrow bay has some rather powerful waves, and the fishermen can be observed toying with their beached boats.

The view from Punta del Teno

Continue westwards along the steep coast. The road – rather tricky to negotiate at first, but well surfaced – leads to the ★★ **Punta del Teno**, a rocky outcrop with a lighthouse (*faro*) on the westernmost point of the island. The view down the coast extends as far as Los Gigantes (*see page 40*) and sometimes even further and the crystal-clear turquoise of the sea contrasts dramatically with the reddish-brown volcanic rock. It's rather difficult to reach the water's edge, but nevertheless the tiny beach here is always crowded at weekends and on public holidays.

Pretty Los Silos

If you don't want to go back the way you came, travel from Buenavista in the direction of **Los Silos**, passing the Montaña de Taco on the left. Los Silos has a very pretty village square and is a good place to stop for coffee. There's also a little church with some interesting 'wedding-cake' dec-

El Tanque

Puerto Santiago

oration. Leave Los Silos now, passing a few extremely beautiful country estates (*fincas*) and banana plantations, and soon what is probably the most homogeneous town on the island, ★ **Garachico**, comes into view, where the remains of the former harbour, most of which was destroyed in a volcanic eruption in 1706, can still be seen. Garachico is described in detail in Route 6 (*see page 61*), so in the meantime take a second view of it from a *mirador* near the junction at the top of the winding road near El Tanque (a short distance away to the east in the direction of Icod). The path taken by the lava from the eruption is clearly visible from here, and Garachico itself looks as if it's been spread out on a drawing-board.

The stretch of road around **El Tanque** has several cheap bars and restaurants (*see page 81*) along it, all of them very popular with the local community. At the end of the village, up on the hillside to the southwest, a cavalcade of patient dromedaries awaits visitors, and riders can even dress up in exotic-looking clothing if they wish.

Those who feel it's still too early to dine should leave El Tanque and head past the large excavated quarries – most of them filled with water – to the ★ **Erjos Pass**, with its superb panoramic view of the Santiago del Teide plateau. The courses taken by the black lava streams are clearly visible from up here. Past Tamaimo, the road goes through a long series of hairpin bends down to the coast, and the resort of **Los Gigantes**. This town, completely overtaken by tourism, is named after the steep, 600-m (2,000-ft) high cliffs nearby called the ★★ **Acantilados de los Gigantes**.

When viewed from above, the town's large, walled-in square of the yachting harbour immediately catches the eye. The restaurants are perfectly situated for a meal at sunset. Los Gigantes is a great deal more peaceful than Las Américas, by the way, and also a bit more homogeneous too. It has a simple, black beach jammed in between the yachting harbour and the steep cliffs, protected by the harbour moles.

The neighbouring tourist centre of **Puerto Santiago**, once a simple fishing village, has a far more pompous beach altogether, the **Playa de la Arena**, which despite its sterility still seems to attract plenty of visitors. The beach has received awards for its cleanliness, but swimmers should beware of the dangerous undertow. From the cliffs above there are fine views of La Gomera.

To get back to Las Américas, return to the coast road, which now passes several wind-shaded banana plantations and the odd urbanisation project. The evening lights of Las Américas soon appear in the distance.

Route 4

Across Mount Teide and Las Cañadas

Puerto de la Cruz – La Orotava – Teide National Park – Vilaflor – Arona – Los Cristianos (90km/55 miles) *See map on page 42*

This route takes us across the middle of Tenerife from the north coast to the south via the island's highest point Mount Teide (3,717m/12,194ft). Impressions here that cannot be provided by any of the other Canary Islands include the weird world of the subalpine crater deserts beneath the mountain, and the seemingly endless lava fields in Las Cañadas. The real highlight of the trip, though, is the sheer experience of climbing Teide itself.

Sometimes the clouds hang above Puerto de la Cruz for days at a time – and this is the best time to climb the majestic mountain. Up on the peak the sun is usually shining. The route passes through La Orotava, the historic starting point for all ascents of the mountain. Explorers in the old days had to employ the services of mules and native porters, who didn't usually share the same scientific interests as their employers. The German scientist Alexander von Humboldt, for instance, discovered when he got back down that the porters had thrown away all the plants and stones he had collected because they had considered them unnecessary ballast!

★★★ **La Orotava** is worth a trip on its own, in fact, just to see the magnificent group of listed buildings at the core of the town, which used to be mainly inhabited by rich nobles and merchants. Ignore the more modern buildings and head straight for the town centre.

Local gossip in La Orotava and the Palacio Municipal

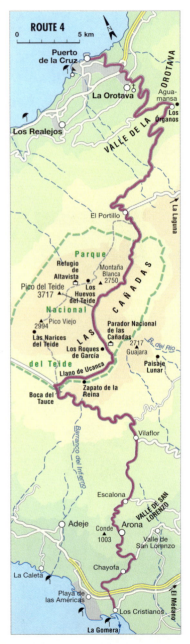

ROUTE 4

0   5 km

Puerto de la Cruz

La Orotava

Los Realejos

VALLE DE LA OROTAVA

Agua-mansa

Los Órganos

La Laguna

El Portillo

Parque

Refugio de Altavista

Montaña Blanca
2750

Pico del Teide
3717

Los Huevos del Teide

Nacional

Pico Viejo
2994

Las Narices del Teide

Los Roques de García

del Teide

Llano de Ucanca

Boca del Tauce

Zapato de la Reina

LAS   CAÑADAS

Parador Nacional de las Cañadas

2717
Guájara

R. del Río

Paisaje Lunar

Barranco del Infierno

Vilaflor

Escalona

VALLE DE SAN LORENZO

Adeje

Conde
1003

Arona

Valle de San Lorenzo

La Caleta

Chayofa

Playa de las Américas

Los Cristianos

El Médano

La Gomera

The Plaza de la Constitución is the town's main square, where the *paseo* (*see page 78*) takes place after the siesta, and there's a good balcony-like observation platform providing a view out across the Orotava Valley, once so famous for its luxuriant vegetation. Today the massive amount of construction work going on is immediately apparent. At the centre of the shady square stands the obligatory pavilion, with its draught beer and coffee machine.

Just before taking a break here, though, pay a quick visit to the church of the former monastery of **San Agustín**, on the northwestern edge of the town, to admire its retables (shelves or frames enclosing decorated panels behind altars) and its Mudéjar-style ceiling. Back in the Plaza, the **Liceo de Taoro**, once a school but now a private club, is still impressively reminiscent of an Italian country estate with its magnificent drive, lined with all manner of blooms.

The Carrera del Escultor Estévez begins just beneath the Plaza, and contains not only the birthplace of the sculptor Fernando Estévez but also the neoclassical **Town Hall** of Villa Orotava, as the town was once called before the parting of the ways with Puerto de la Cruz. During the Corpus Christi celebrations, religious pictures made of pastel-coloured volcanic soil and blossom, which have been carefully assembled days in advance, are put on display. Behind the Town Hall, the **Hijuelo del Botánico**, a smaller version of the Botanical Gardens in Puerto de la Cruz, contains quite a number of tropical and subtropical plants. Unfortunately most of the magnificent blossom can only be observed through a fence.

The religious centre of Orotava is the baroque ★ **Church of Nuestra Señora de la Concepción**. Its twin towers and the central dome towering above them are a landmark for the most architecturally interesting part of the old town. The church contains several good examples of Canarian wood-carving and there are two sculptures by Luján Pérez, who was born here, and two by Fernando Estévez. The Pérez statues are of a *Mater Dolorosa* and *St John*, those by Estévez are *Candelaria* and *St Peter*. The neoclassical marble pulpit is Genoese, and the marble tabernacle on the main altar is by the Italian master Giuseppe Gagini. There are also two very good paintings: *The Marriage of the Virgin Mary to St Joseph* by Cristóbal Quintana, and an *Immaculate Conception* by Gaspar de Quevedo.

The street continues steeply upwards, passing several old town houses once occupied by noble families. The **Casa de los Balcones**, which was built in 1632, soon comes into view on the left-hand side. The *patio* and rooms of this stately house are now salesrooms containing various displays of Canarian handicraft, particularly lace. The same applies to the building opposite, the **Casa de la Alfombra**, which dates from 1590. A few yards further up is the massive complex of the **Hospital de la Santísima Trinidad** (Holy Trinity Hospital), which was once a convent. There's still a cradle in the entrance which was used by young mothers when they abandoned their babies into the care of the Franciscan nuns. Below is a cemetery with several interesting old tomb slabs set into its walls.

The Church of San Augustín and Casa de los Balcones

Above the hospital is the former mill district known as **El Farrobo**. Those with enough strength to go the extra way will recognise the old mills above their now disused waterways which once channelled the water to the wheels. Several millers still possess their ancient *gofio* (roast maize flour, *see page 81*) mills even though they are no longer used, and are happy to show them to interested visitors with time on their hands.

43

Between the mill district and the Plaza de la Constitución is a series of terraced gardens which have recently been renovated. This public park, the ★ **Jardín Victoria**, contains the Carrara marble mausoleum of Diego Ponte del Castillo, designed by the French architect Adolphe Coquet in 1882. The view of the old part of La Orotava from the mausoleum is the best in town.

Below the Plaza de la Constitución, the tower of the church of Santo Domingo can be seen. Once a Dominican monastery, two floors inside have been given over to a very well-presented ★ **Museum of Spanish-American Crafts**. The musical instrument collection is particularly good, and the museum also contains ceramics, basketwork and a small selection of furniture. The **Casa Torrehermosa** on the opposite side of the street has salesrooms with various island crafts on offer. The building itself dates from the 17th century and has recently been renovated.

View across the Orotava Valley

Leave La Orotava now by its eastern, more modern section and follow signs to Las Cañadas. The road follows a series of long bends as it climbs the valley slope, passing several hamlets. Around 1,000m (3,280ft) up, just below where the pine forest layer starts, is ★★ **Aguamansa**, famed for its large trout and carp farm, which is open to visitors. A section of forest nearby has been turned into a nature trail, where the trees have all been labelled, and there is also a series of aviaries – a kind of 'bird refuge'. Injured or rejected birds are given temporary or permanent accommodation here.

Visitors who park their cars next to the fish farm and get their bearings from a detailed map of the area will discover a series of very attractive walks. One particularly good one is to **Los Organos**, a high rock wall with enormous basalt pillars reminiscent of organ pipes. The whole forest above the Orotava Valley is full of well-marked paths and hiking routes. There are also several shelters in which to take refuge in the event of heavy rain. Since most of this area is inside the cloud layer and can often get quite foggy, it's a good idea to take along protective clothing, and *never* come here without a good map. With the amount of lichen growing up here, it's obvious how regularly this forest is bathed in cloud.

Further along the way to Las Cañadas, look out for a very noticeable basalt 'flower' on the left-hand side of the road, between kilometre stones 22 and 23. The *Tinerfeños* have dubbed this remarkable rock formation *Marguerita de Piedra*.

Information kiosk and restaurant at El Portillo

Near El Portillo, which is just a small collection of houses with a first-aid centre and a fire station, the ★★★ **Teide National Park** begins, as does ★★★ **Las Cañadas**, the name given to the floor of an ancient volcano strewn with smaller volcanic cones. Its elliptical *caldera* (sunken crater) is 17km (10 miles) long and 11km (7 miles) across, making it one of the largest in the world. A **Visitor Centre** situated between El Portillo and a series of bars and restaurants (El Portillo Alto) has display cases, brochures and also a multimedia show explaining the various special features of the nature reserve.

Opposite the centre, hikers can take a 13-km (8-mile) long route signposted to Siete Cañadas, ending at the state-run Parador Nacional hotel. It's not difficult as far as ascents and descents are concerned, getting your bearings is simple, but the heat, the distance and the altitude may cause problems – sturdy footwear, a detailed map, sun protection and enough to drink are all essential. Anyone who wants to do a bit of *moufflon* spotting (it's a famously shaggy sheep) will need binoculars and a great deal of patience. This hike is especially good between May and July, when the landscape is covered with a carpet of flowers. The air is full of the sound of bees – and the honey they produce is utterly delicious.

Even when seen from the main road, the lava tells its own story. Particularly rough and bizarrely shaped surfaces have been produced by lava with a higher gas content, and the shiny, black, glassy surfaces mark the areas that cooled rapidly without having time to crystallize. This black substance is known as obsidian, and the Guanches used it to make axe blades. Large sections of Las Cañadas are covered with tiny cones made of porous pumice stone, varying in colour from turquoise to reddish-brown. The stone's water-absorbent properties seem to have been well known to the Guanches, who covered their fields with layers of it. This technique is still employed in the Canary Islands today (*see pages 48 and 66*).

The **Montaña Blanca** is one such pumice cone. Its base is 2,300m (7,545ft) above sea level, and usually forms the starting point for climbs up ★★★ **Mount Teide** (3,717m/ 12,194ft), the highest mountain in the Canarian archipelago and in all Spain as well.

Teide's lunar landscape

The mountain is thought to be relatively young, just 600,000 years old, in fact. As can be seen from its shape, it was formed in a series of earth movements. First there was the enormous original volcano, the top of which either blew off or – more likely – collapsed back into itself. Next, the small volcano next to Teide, the **Pico Viejo**, sprung up and was then followed by the enormous cone of Teide itself, attaining a height of around 3,600m (11,810ft). One final eruption gave Teide its tiny hat. In contrast to the Pico Viejo, the Teide crater is rather less impressive at just a mere 30m (98ft) deep. Sulphurous fumes and vapours escape continuously from the small cracks in the rock in and around the crater, exuding at a temperature of around 85°C (185°F). These vapours make the ascent even more breathtaking.

45

While the final route to summit above the cable car station (*see page 46*) is normally closed, hikers who arrive before the first cable car and accompanying guards at 9am can still get to the top of the mountain. It is imperative that they take along sturdy footwear, warm clothing (it can get very windy up near the peak), sun protection, enough provisions and torches with spare batteries. Those planning to stay the night in the Altavista hut should also take a

The road through Teide

sleeping bag. Those travelling by car, who will have parked down at the turn-off to Montaña Blanca, should make absolutely sure they've left no valuables inside the vehicle. Seemingly, isolated mountain regions are the most likely place for cars to be broken into.

The ascent begins in a broad arc around the Montaña Blanca, and carries on comfortably uphill to an altitude of 2,800m (9,186ft), passing large black chunks of volcanic rock known as *Huevos del Teide* (Teide Eggs). Then for the next hour and a half the going gets steeper. The Estancia de los Ingleses and de los Alemanes, two boulder-strewn ledges, break the journey and provide welcome resting places. At 3,300m (10,826ft) the Altavista hut comes into view (there's no proper food up here, just drink and maybe soup). Anyone intending to spend the night here can hire an ancient bunk with a squeaky misshapen mattress comparatively cheaply. It is worth staying the night up here to experience the sunrise and to watch the movement of Teide's shadow from the peak.

Two hours before dawn, most of the contorted sleepers awake and continue along the path by torchlight, which is quite easy, and one hour later the cable-car terminus (3,600m/11,800ft) comes into view. The cable car is the simpler way to ascend the mountain, of course, but in peak season (if you'll excuse the pun) expect to have to wait for up to two hours. The two cable cars (daily 9am–4pm), which travel in opposite directions, cover an altitude difference of 1,200m (3,936ft) in just eight minutes, but in windy weather the service doesn't operate. As mentioned on page 45, those who wish to accept the challenge of reaching the summit under their own steam should be past the terminus before the first cable car arrives. From here, the steep ascent takes about half an hour. If there's a strong wind it can get quite dangerous, because the route crosses several exposed drops. The whole island can be seen from the top, along with Gran Canaria, El Hierro, La Gomera and La Palma which, more often than not, look as if they are floating in the orange-tinted clouds far below.

The easy way up the mountain

Los Roques de García

46

One of the main attractions in Las Cañadas is the row of rocks opposite the Parador Nacional hotel known as ★★ **Los Roques de García**. They separate the higher part of Las Cañadas plateau from its lower section, and are the eroded remains of volcanic rock which have been partially preserved due to a harder protective layer. Nearby the rocks are tinted with turquoise due to copper oxide and are known as **Los Azulejos**. From here there are sweeping views across dark lava that spreads towards a former lake, **Llano de Ucanca**. This flat and decidedly featureless desert-like plain is often used as scenery in science fiction films.

The Parador Nacional (*see page 44*) is the only place that provides long-term accommodation of any kind in this region – and its prices and service aren't always that excellent. There was even talk of closing it down at one stage, but now it's undergoing an expensive facelift. The hotel is 2,100m (6,890ft) above sea level and is a very good starting point for any hikes in the region.

A hike to the top of the ★★ **Guajara**, the highest point on the rim of the ancient crater, is particularly recommended, as is an excursion into the ★★ **Paisaje Lunar** (Lunar Landscape) via the slightly less steep side of the Guajara. It's essential to have a detailed map for this latter hike, because if banks of cloud start rolling in from the south it is easy to lose your bearings.

On the way there, in the direction of Vilaflor near Boca de Tauce, there's a relatively low-altitude rock formation on the left called The Princess's Shoe and looking at it, it's easy to see the rough outline of a high-heeled shoe. Soon the pine forest gets a lot denser and mightier and just before Vilaflor, at kilometre stone 65, a broad and bumpy forest track leads off to the left to the summer camp of Madre del Agua, 8km (5 miles) away. From here it's just another half hour on foot to the Lunar Landscape. Wind erosion has created this amazing area in a ravine. The spicy smell of pines, which are very gnarled-looking indeed, fills the air and adds to the atmosphere.

★★ **Vilaflor** is 1,400m (4,593ft) above sea level, and is believed to be the highest village in all the Canary Islands. Well known for its good air, it also produces a very healthy bottled mineral water straight from the source. In the past, Vilaflor was also famous for its lace, and the women of the village used to make several valuable textiles by hand, with black lace *mantillas* (veils) as their speciality. These days it's hard to find such workmanship and most of the

Los Roques de García and the Parador Nacional

Taking the plunge in Los Cristianos...

objects on offer are factory-made products. The crop cultivation up here (grapevines, potatoes and tomatoes) is done on a series of terraces, using pumice stone. For a view of the area from above, go up to the hermitage on the other side of the *barranco*, where there's also a good restaurant called El Mirador.

Continuing southwards, the next large village is **Arona**, which like Adeje has profited from the agglomeration around Los Cristianos – the new Town Hall, built in the Canarian style, is just one example. In the church on the square, don't miss one of the finest retables (*see page 75*) in Spain.

Those who haven't had dinner yet and would like to sample good regional cooking should consider doing so at this point, before entering tourist food territory again. Anyone here during the daytime should visit the Ecology Park, ★ **Las Aguilas de Teide** (daily 9am–7pm), just below Arona, with its tropical greenery and birds of prey, crocodiles and penguins.

...and going dolphin-watching

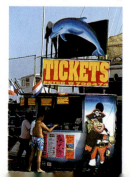

Pass through the Urbanisación Chayofa, a lush oasis in the wilderness, and soon ★ **Los Cristianos** comes into view. Similar to Las Américas, though perhaps slightly less hectic, Los Cristianos also used to be a fishing village before the boom in tourism, and some *Tinerfeños* do still fish from here. From the harbour there's a car ferry and speedboat service to La Gomera; a windjammer offers trips up and down the coast and several boats can also be hired for dolphin-watching.

The sandy beach and the bay are protected by a jetty so that children can bathe in safety. A new cultural centre on the General Franco puts on modern art exhibitions and shows prizewinning films.

Route 5

The evergreen mountains of the Anaga

La Laguna – Las Mercedes – Cruz del Carmen – Pico del Inglés – Taganana – San Andres – Santa Cruz de Tenerife

From La Laguna, the archipelago's former capital and still its spiritual centre, this route follows several steep and winding roads across a mountain massif which is covered with large areas of laurel forest. Clouds permitting, the trip provides the visitor with a whole series of breathtaking views across ravines, mountain ridges, steep coasts and offshore islands.

Founded by the conquistador Alonso Fernandez de Lugo in 1496, ★★ **La Laguna** had to relinquish its role as capital of the Canary Islands in 1723, in favour of the economically more prosperous Santa Cruz and is now the second most important town on Tenerife. Almost 100 years later, La Laguna became an episcopal see and was given a permanent university. Life in the town clearly reflects both these historical facts. Nowhere else on the island are church and university festivities celebrated with such solemnity and splendour as they are here, and nowhere

La Laguna: the university

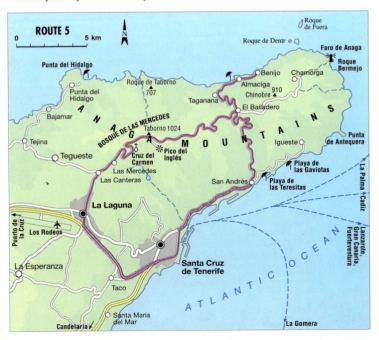

else is the atmosphere as communicative, friendly and relaxed as it is in the student bars in the Barrio Nuevo. There's a real authenticity about La Laguna, and the town is a fascinating mixture of cosmopolitanism and self-sufficiency. Situated just 8km (5 miles) inland from the centre of the capital, La Laguna enjoys a cooler climate than coastal areas, which helps contribute to the attractions of living in this historic place.

Walk down the streets of La Laguna during siesta time and the town can look very remote and forbidding indeed. In the old part of town, there are hardly any windows in the walls of the former monasteries such as **Santa Clara** in the Calle de Viana or **Santa Catalina** in the **Plaza del Adelantado**, the town's main square. All life seems to come to a halt during the midday heat, and the only signs of interest in the outside world are the balconies outside the old houses and monasteries, several of which overlook the central plaza.

Southwest of the Santa Catalina monastery is the neo-classical Town Hall, built in 1822, with its unpretentious loggia. The building housing the municipal archives on the left of it is decorated with neo-Gothic and plant ornamentation. The most historically important secular structure in La Laguna, however, is the **Palacio de Nava y Grimón** at the northwestern end of the plaza to the right of Santa Catalina. Construction work on this building with its dark-grey baroque facade began in 1590. The portico is flanked by double columns. The Nava y Grimón family used to be among the most important on the island.

On the eastern side of the square is the **market**, with several halls beyond it, which is particularly famed for the quality of its herbs. The former hermitage of San Miguel, to the right of it, constructed by order of Alonso de Lugo now houses an **art gallery** (Sunday 11am–1pm, Mon-

Balconies are beautifully carved

Flower arrangement at the market

Palacio de Nava y Grimón

day 5–8pm, Tuesday to Saturday 11am–1pm and 5–8pm). On the southeastern side is the birthplace of Padre José de Anchieta, who did much missionary work in Brazil and is widely believed to have founded the city of São Paolo.

Walk slightly downhill away from the square in a southerly direction to the former Dominican **monastery of Santo Domingo**. A monastery school founded here in the 16th century for the study of grammar, logic and philosophy was the forerunner of today's **university**. The interior of the church is dominated by a colourful fresco painted by Mariano de Cossío in 1948. The monastery garden is rather neglected, but it does contain a magnificent old dragon tree. Nearby is the neo-Canarian university administration building.

The main shopping street in La Laguna is the Obispo Rey Redondo, which begins on the Plaza del Adelantado. It leads past the house behind the Ayuntiamento (Town Hall) known as the **Casa de los Capitanes**, which was the seat of several military governors during the 18th century and is now used as an exhibition centre (Monday to Saturday 11am–1pm and 5–8pm).

Halfway along the Obispo Rey Redondo is Laguna's ★ **Cathedral**, which has undergone much alteration over the centuries, receiving its present-day appearance at the beginning of the 20th century. The neoclassical facade dates from 1820, though. Behind the main altar inside is the simple tomb of the town's founder and Tenerife's conqueror, Alonso de Lugo. The decoration on the retable (*see page 75*) also merits attention, as it was by Van Dyck's teacher Hendrick van Balen. The tabernacle at the main altar is the work of Luján Pérez, and the majestic painting of *Souls in Purgatory* is by Canarian artist Cristóbal de Quintana. This interior is at its most magnificent on high holidays, when the gold and silverwork on the retable reflects the candlelight.

The Obispo Rey Redondo continues straight to the church of ★★ **Nuestra Señora de la Concepción**, which has been declared a national shrine. The interior boasts a polychromatic ceiling in the Mudéjar style and a glazed font dating from the 15th century. The magnificent wooden pulpit with its elaborate carvings is by an anonymous artist and the choir stalls are very impressive. There's also a *Predilecta* (Chosen Virgin) by Luján Pérez, and a painting of the church's patron saint by Fernando Estévez.

After visiting the church, drop into the nearby baker's shop – López Echeto, at San Antonio 16 – with its delicious bread, cakes and confectionery, considered by many locals to be the best on the island.

The best route back to the Plaza del Adelantado is via the San Agustín, because there are several more sights to see along it. The first of these is the **Institute of**

La Laguna locals

51

Nuestra Señora de Concepción

Canarian Studies, at present being renovated. The building dates from the early 16th century and has one of the finest *patios* on the island. By the way, beyond it to the east is a very attractive palm-lined avenue with benches (upon which to enjoy freshly purchased cake). The monastery of **San Agustín** is no more than a stately ruin, but in contrast, the baroque **Palacio Episcopal**, with its enormous barred windows, is still in good condition. This palace was originally a gentlemen's club, and it was at the piano here that the famous Canarian composer Teobaldo Power wrote his *Cantos Canarios*.

A short distance away is the Late Renaissance Casa Lercaro, built in 1593. Today it houses the **Museo de Historia de Tenerife** (Tuesday to Saturday 10am-5pm, Sunday 10am–2pm). The exhibits here concentrate on the period of Spanish occupation from the beginnings of the *Conquista* to the present.

There's also a fascinating museum dedicated to space and science on the outskirts of the town on the way to Santa Cruz. The ★★ **Museo de la Ciencia y el Cosmos** (Tuesday to Sunday 10am–8pm, Wednesday admission free) has all kinds of buttons to press, along with computers, film rooms, and a planetarium, all documenting natural phenomena.

The Anaga Mountains

Now it's back to nature, but try not to leave La Laguna during the rush hour, when it becomes one very unpleasant traffic jam. La Laguna is the gateway to the **Anaga Mountains**, a sweeping rampart of volcanic peaks that fills the northeast corner of Tenerife, and the main route into this thinly populated area is punctuated by a succession of stunning observation points (*miradores*).

Either follow the signs to Las Mercedes or to Bajamar (and Las Mercedes). On the latter route, take the turn-off into the village of **Las Canteras**. The forest near **Las Mercedes** contains some of the finest laurels in the Canary Islands. Further along the road are several good places to stop and enjoy the view. The **Mirador Jardín** and **Cruz del Carmen** (car park) both provide excellent views across the La Laguna plateau as far as Teide.

Those keen to explore the western Anaga on foot should begin their hike in Cruz del Carmen (Transmersa bus access from La Laguna). A four hour-long, medium-difficulty hike leads via **Las Carboneras** (a former mining community) and **Chinamada** (cave dwellings) to **Punta del Hidalgo** (*see Route 6, page 55*). The trip back to La Laguna can be done by TITSA bus. The route is (fairly) well signposted and begins right opposite the *mirador*; passing through a stretch of forest that's very reminiscent of a jungle, and ending up in a drier, cactus-filled region near the coast.

From about 11am onwards, Cruz del Carmen is often covered by cloud, which of course makes visibility difficult. The same applies to the ★★ **Pico del Inglés**, which has one of the best views on the whole island. Its name is said to derive from the days when English buccaneers who roamed the surrounding seas had a lookout at this strategic spot to signal whenever a vessel was nearby. The view northwards from here extends across everything that has been visible from the *miradores* so far, plus the whole of the Anaga – from the Punta del Hidalgo in the west to the islands off the coast to the east known as the Roques de Anaga. Clouds can actually add even more majesty to the scene, and photographers should note that cloud movement is particularly intensive around **El Bailadero**, a gusty and cool area where its best to wear a weatherproof jacket. By the way, the small restaurant under the ridge here makes an excellent chickpea soup known locally as *sopa de garbanzas*. Visitors of a nervous disposition should note that El Bailadero has long been regarded as a meeting place for witches.

Clouds roll in at El Bailadero

53

The nearby village of **Taganana** produces its own wine, which tastes very good but is also extremely strong (17 percent alcohol) – so those driving should avoid it. Taganana has retained its simplicity, despite the fact that some of its restaurants are making concessions to tourism. Agriculturally, the region is still semi-feudal, as farms are rented out in exchange for half the produce, and their tenants are referred to as *medianeros*. The soil is fertile and the yield in good years can be anywhere between 25 and 35 times as much as what was originally sown.

Although the Anaga contains numerous tiny terraced fields, large parts of the massif are only suitable for grazing herds of goats. Hikers often encounter goatherds,

Pico del Inglés provides one of the best views on the island

dressed in woollen capes, guiding their animals across the difficult terrain. They still carry the goat-leather pouches known as *zurrones*, containing wine, water and *gofio* (roast maize flour, *see page 81*). The odd rabbit is hunted to supplement their diet. To catch rabbits, the hunters on Tenerife not only use rifles but also ferrets. The animals are kept inside longish boxes, and drive the rabbits out of their warrens straight into the hunters' line of fire.

Beneath Taganana there is a beach and a good fresh fish restaurant called the Playa, offering *pulpo frito* (fried squid). There are several other small restaurants (and quite a few very stony beaches) along the coast between here and Benijo.

Anyone in a car, as opposed to public transport, who wants to explore the eastern Anaga on foot can make a detour to **Chamorga** from El Bailadero, and go on a five-hour strenuous hike from there. The trek back to Chamorga passes through **El Dragillo**, where there's a very fine dragon tree, **Las Palmas**, where many of the abandoned old houses are now inhabited by back-to-nature enthusiasts (*see page 12*), and **Roque Bermejo** with its lighthouse. Along the way there's also a good close-up view of the Roques de Anaga (bring along binoculars, though), with their colony of stormy petrels. At the end the path goes uphill through a fairly long *barranco*.

Playa de las Teresitas

Long before it gets dark, why not make your way to ★ **Playa de las Teresitas**, the liveliest beach in Tenerife (the sand has been imported from the Sahara). To get there, drive in the direction of Santa Cruz, via San Andrés. The road winds its way down the southern slopes of the Anaga in a rather dizzying series of hairpins, and the vegetation quickly alters in appearance. The lush green becomes a brownish-yellow, and cacti and palm trees dot the landscape. The road finally arrives at **San Andrés** with its excellent beach. A harbour mole and a series of breakwaters protect the fishing boats, the sandy beach and the swimmers from the open sea. Palm trees have been planted to provide shade, the restaurants and bars are well stocked with food and drink, and there are showers placed at regular intervals along the beach. Try the local seafood restaurants here. The fish is usually fresh, but to be absolutely sure, choose a restaurant where you can select from the live fish swimming in a large aquarium outside.

Round off the day with a visit to Santa Cruz de Tenerife (*see page 18*) for a stroll down the Rambla del General Franco and a relaxing evening drink in the Plaza de la Paz. Alternatively, there are several good bars back in La Laguna (*see page 49*).

Route 6

A bird's eye view of craggy coasts

Punta del Hidalgo – Tejina – Valle de Guerra – Tacoronte – El Sauzal – Santa Ursula – Los Realejos – Icod de los Vinos – Garachico (75km/46 miles) *See map on pages 56–7*

The green northern part of Tenerife is an irregular series of rough promontories, often reaching far out into the sea, bizarre-looking, precipitous cliffs and broad, welcoming valleys. The villages and hamlets cling precariously to the steep slopes, while the *valles* – assuming they haven't been earmarked for real estate – are farmed very intensively. This route provides a view of the coastline from above.

The northeast of Tenerife seems to be entirely a German holiday enclave. The signs in Punta del Hidalgo, for instance, are in both German and Spanish, and the bar and restaurant staff usually speak both languages too. ★ **Punta del Hidalgo** is one of the best starting points for hikes into the Anaga. For example, from the eastern end of the main street, near the monument to Canarian crooner Sebastián Ramos, known familiarly as *El Puntero* (a derivative of Punta del Hidalgo, where he used to perform regularly), there's a medium-difficult hike to the still inhabited cave dwellings of ★ **Chinamada**. Here the white houses squatting on ledges above the sheer *barranco* look just the same as any other mountain farms, it's only when you get closer you realise that the doors and windows are set into the rock face with the living quarters extending into caves behind.

The resort area has two sea-water bathing pools. Local people maintain that sunsets here are the most spectacular on Tenerife.

Punta del Hidalgo

Puerto de la Cruz · Santa Cruz de Tenerife

55

Inspecting the sand at Playa de San Marcos

Bajamar

The rum distillery at Tejina

Just after the village name-sign at the entrance to **Bajamar** on the right, there's a very good café that does German cakes and coffee. In the village itself, public life has an elderly slowness to it, and tends to revolve around the central sea-water swimming pool. On sunny weekends the place is livened up by an influx of younger people.

On the eastern edge of the Valle de Guerra, **Tejina** has devoted itself almost entirely to agriculture. The main crop here is bananas, but flowers are also grown. On the right-hand side just past the centre of the village is a rum distillery. Sugar cane is no longer grown in Tejina, but rum is produced just the same, and the distillery can produce up to 70,000 litres a day during the three-month annual season. Other alcoholic beverages are produced here too, including the popular *ron miel* (honey rum), and also a banana liqueur (*see Food & Drink, page 81*).

Valle de Guerra, named after a military leader in the Spanish *Conquista*, is also an agricultural centre like Tejina. There's a scientific agricultural institute here, a short distance outside the village, providing the local farmers with help and advice on how to diversify their crops. Just a few steps away from the institute, on the opposite side of the road, is an interesting ★ **Ethnographical Museum** housed inside a magnificent old *finca* (country estate), the Casa de Carta, with exhibits documenting daily life in the Canary Islands.

On the way to Tacoronte there's a good detour to ★ **El Pris** (4.5km/3 miles). Despite the presence of a few rows of modern apartments up in the rocks here, the lives of the local fisherfolk have hardly changed over the years. When the men return with the catch the women help them to wind

the boats in. Nearby **Mesa del Mar** is mostly a tourist centre, with some pretty sterile architecture, all of it situated beneath a spectacular section of steep coastline.

Despite the variety of agriculture in and around ★ **Tacoronte**, the town is famous most of all for its wine. The surrounding villages are all members of the Tacoronte-Acentejo winegrowers' association, and produce quality wines. Those keen to try out the various types that the Canary Islands have to offer should go to the tasting hall at the *Bodegas Alvaro*, the largest wine dealer on Tenerife, where on two floors there's a fine selection of the archipelago's greatest wines (*see Food & Drink, page 81*). The building is located 2km (1 mile) outside the centre on the road to La Laguna (daily 9am–1pm and 3–6pm).

The busy town has two churches. The three-aisled 16th-century parish **Church of Santa Catalina** contains two of the most important altarpieces in Tenerife – the *Immaculate Conception* retable in the left-hand side-aisle, and the retable of the *Sagrado Corazon*. There's also a good *Immaculada* by Luján Pérez, and *Santa Catalina* by a Seville master. The simpler **Santísimo Cristo de los Dolores**, a former monastery, has a remarkable carved figure of Christ standing beside the cross, brought here from Madrid in 1662 (it's on display in the Santa Catalina church at present because of renovation work).

Enjoying the view at El Sauzal

The centre of **El Sauzal** further along the coast has really been spruced up. There's a miniature version of the flight of steps in Eisenstein's *Battleship Potemkin* leading up to the town's neo-Canarian Town Hall. Nearby, a small artificial waterfall splashes away happily in the tropical garden outside the building. From above there's a good view of the **Church of San Pedro** with its Moorish-look-

Church of San Pedro

Evening drinks in La Victoria

ing dome. The silhouette of the coast can be seen far away in the distance.

The region on the other side of the northern motorway near Acentejo, where islanders keep themselves to themselves in small, inconspicuous wine bars called *Guachinches*, is steeped in history. This is where the decisive early battles were fought between the Spanish and the Tenerife's original inhabitants. The village of **La Matanza de Acentejo** (The Battle of Acentejo) is a reminder of the day on which Spanish forces (and some Guanche troops they had persuaded to join them) suffered a serious defeat in the nearby *barrancos*. Of an original army of 1,200, only 200 – including Alonso Fernández de Lugo – escaped with their lives.

Legend has it that the Guanches (*see page 15*) allowed their enemies to penetrate deep inside their territory and made a present to them of some cattle. They then whistled to the animals behind the Spanish lines and in the ensuing confusion carried out their counter-attack. Spears, boulders and wooden stakes rained down on to the Spaniards from high up in the *barrancos*. This victory gave the Guanches one year's breathing space, but then de Lugo returned with reinforcements and conquered them on the high plateau of La Laguna. He never managed to totally subjugate them, however.

Their ranks severely thinned, the Guanches were soon weakened still further by an outbreak of the plague, and on Christmas Day 1495 they were forced to concede total defeat at **La Victoria de Acentejo**. Thousands were murdered that day, but the battle was considered a victory and explains how the village got its glorious name. A wind-blown pine tree next to the church above the main road is said to date from the days of Alonso de Lugo.

La Victoria: the local cemetery

The church itself has an artistic ceiling in the Mudéjar style and a Portuguese-colonial main chapel. An old lady in this village still makes pots as the Guanches used to, ie without the use of a wheel. Whether any of the younger people will follow her example remains to be seen.

Like the nearby Orotava Valley, the long, drawn-out village of **Santa Ursula** is home to many long-term residents from central and northwestern Europe. The whole place looks very prosperous, with a flourishing wine trade and leather industry, and it attracts a lot of day-trippers from Puerto de la Cruz. The road to La Orotava passes the spot about which the famous German explorer Alexander von Humboldt (*see page 12*), impressed by the view, wrote years later that he had 'never been faced by a more varied, attractive scene, with such a harmonious distribution of rock and greenery, anywhere in this world'.

At the *mirador* which bears his name, it's still possible to see what must have prompted the statement. Take away the banana plantations and all the modern buildings and add lots of floral variety, and it's possible to imagine how the island must once have looked. In the café here named after the great explorer, the view can be enjoyed with some good coffee and cake.

To reach **Los Realejos**, go through La Orotava (*see Route 4, page 41*) – unless you feel like admiring the Orotava Valley from above, in which case start off by following signs to Las Cañadas, which will lead you through the eastern built-up area of La Orotava. After about 8km (5 miles) of twists and turns, the road reaches a turn-off to Los Realejos via Palo Blanco. It's clear that what is grown up here has to be pretty robust to stand the climate, so potatoes, maize and other cereals predominate.

Realejo Alto, the upper part of town and also the oldest, is where the last organised Guanche resistance was finally crushed in 1496. The ★ **oldest church on Tenerife** was built on the site of Alonso de Lugo's military camp in 1498, and was consecrated to Santiago, the patron saint of Spain. The Guanches who preferred conversion to Christianity to a far worse fate were first baptised here, and later in La Laguna as well. The church has been altered many times, and not much remains of the original structure. The choir at the main altar is mid-17th century; the statue of Christ is by Martín de Andújar and there is also a *Santa Lucía* from Flanders.

From the new Town Hall nearby, there's a very good view across the valley. On the other side of a *barranco* below, is a cemetery with one of the most symmetrical-looking dragon trees on the island. Los Realejos also boasts a famous son – José de Viera y Clavijo, the first proper chronicler of Canarian history, was born here in 1731. His

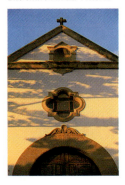
The church in La Victoria

Resting the legs

Tenerife's oldest church: door detail

59

Noticias de la Historia General de las Islas Canarias has been the official work of reference for the past two centuries. An enlightened theologian and a friend of Voltaire and other free thinkers, Clavijo died in Las Palmas in 1813.

The lower part of Realejo (Bajo) is almost entirely modern. A council house construction programme has successfully avoided slum development. The strip of coastline beneath the motorway has been completely taken over by the tourist industry. Several hotels in amongst the banana plantations are actually quite romantic. The beach at **El Socorro** is popular with surfers whenever the wind gets up, but swimming there can be quite dangerous because of the undertow.

Locals of La Guancha

La Guancha lies on the steep slope of the **Ladera de Tigaiga**. It forms a good counterpart to the Humboldt view, and the built-up areas down in the valley are even more noticeable. According to legend, it was from the edge of the Ladera that Bentor, the son of the *Mencey* (prince) of Taoro, threw himself to his death after the defeat of the Guanches at La Victoria de Acentejo. Such death leaps were by no means rare among the Guanches if the traditional stories are to be believed. Whenever a new *mencey* (*see page 15*) was appointed, sons of poor parents would often sacrifice themselves in this way to ensure that their family was supported for a lifetime by the new ruler.

Those who throw themselves off the edges of the ravines round here these days are attached to hang-gliders, and usually land in one piece down on the Playa Jardín in Puerto.

San Juan de Rambla: detail

Like Realejo Bajo, La Guancha is a very modern-looking place with scarcely a historic building in sight. **San Juan de la Rambla** (3km/2 miles), on the other hand, is a beautiful white village next to the sea, with a very pretty centre. The winding alleys near the church contain quite a few old-style Canarian wooden balconies made of pine. A less attractive aspect of the place is its unemployment rate – the highest on the island.

★★ **Icod de los Vinos** is one of the most visited towns on Tenerife, less for its old buildings than for its legendary ★★★ **dragon tree**. Known as *El Drago*, or *El Drago Milenario*, it stands on the western edge of the town and is included in Icod's coat of arms. Despite all its concrete and metal supports, this ancient tree is still very much alive, but its age is somewhat questionable. Although the dragon tree of the Canary Islands is a relic from the Tertiary period, this particular specimen at Icod may not even be 1,000 years old, but probably dates from the days of the *Conquista* at the earliest.

The dragon tree

But Icod doesn't just boast the dragon tree, the church square provides a view of all kinds of different specimens of the island's flora. You can stroll through Canary pine, palm trees, jacaranda trees and ornamental bananas. The Canarian laurel can also be admired here. As far as buildings are concerned, Icod's parish ★ **Church of San Marcos** contains a very fine 17th-century retable and impressive Mudéjar style ceilings above all three of its aisles. The sacristy (Monday to Saturday 9am–12.30pm) containing the church treasure is a small museum in its own right. Alongside religious clothing and liturgical instruments, there is also a particularly magnificent exhibit of a cross made of Mexican silver. It weighs 47 kilos and is 2m (6 feet) high, and is considered to be the finest work of silver filigree ever made.

Church of San Marcos

The Plaza de la Constitución a bit further uphill is lined by buildings with balconies typical of the island. At the centre of the square is an attractive moss-covered fountain and wine lovers will find it interesting to visit the Casa del Vino Canario.

Just below Icod is **Playa de San Marcos** which is a good spot to go for a refreshing swim. The black lava beach is surrounded by rocks, and there are several restaurants here too, with a handful of fishing boats and some local swimmers giving the place a flair of its own.

San Marcos fishing boats

61

The final destination on this route is the immaculate little town of ★ **Garachico**, which presents a rare picture of architectural unity. Apart from a few modern buildings along the coast road, which hardly spoil the overall effect, this once prosperous harbour town has retained its almost medieval aspect. Founded by the Genoese family of Ponte in 1499, Garachico rose to become the most important harbour on the island during the years follow-

Surfing at San Marcos

Immaculate Garachico

The Church of Santa Ana

62

Castillo de San Miguel

ing the *Conquista*. The main export shipped from the town was the Malmsey wine produced in the northern part of the island which was once *de rigueur* in English and European society drawing rooms.

Several catastrophes, including plague epidemics, floods, landslides and fires arrested the town's development to such an extent during the 17th century that the harbours at Santa Cruz and La Orotava (Puerto de la Cruz) stepped in as rivals. Garachico was finished as a port once and for all in 1706, when two rivers of lava flowing down from the erupted Pico Viejo on Mount Teide buried the harbour basin and destroyed most of the surrounding buildings. The **Church of Santa Ana**, with its valuable retable by the Martín de Andujár school, was spared because of its slightly higher position, but everything to the west of it was buried beneath the molten lava. However, some of the buildings in Garachico today still retain sections dating from before the eruption. The former entrance to the harbour is now a little park, and the old harbour gate has been excavated. At the back of this small complex, there's an interesting old winepress.

The story goes that the reason for the disaster was an evil monk, who was a personal chaplain to an aristocratic family in Garachico. The monk had become so influential that he was akin to a tyrant, dictating to and dominating the household. Eventually the lord and master gave him his marching orders and he left. But as he went, he cursed the townspeople, who all knew about his humiliation, and a few days later the volcano erupted.

On the Plaza de Arriba, beyond Santa Ana, the attractive former **Convento de San Francisco** on the other side of the square has been given a facelift and now fulfils the role of Town Hall, a cultural centre, exhibition rooms and the municipal library. Outside, the statue of the liberator Simón Bolívar recalls the fact that his mother was born here. Note the *patios* surrounded by balconies which are such a typical feature of Canarian architecture. Two streets further to the north is another convent, this time still in use. The Franciscan nuns are separated from their visitors by small grilles. The monastery of **Santo Domingo** at the entrance to the town has now been converted into an old people's home, but it also contains an interesting collection of modern art (Museo de Arte, Monday to Saturday 9.30am–6pm).

The small **Castillo de San Miguel** down by the sea makes a good place to stop and relax at the end of the route, with its sea-water swimming pool, a restaurant with a beautiful view out to sea, and a series of attractive and inviting places to sit and enjoy a coffee or a beer. From the castle's roof the two rivers of lava can clearly be seen solidified on the hillside.

Route 7

The Cumbre Dorsal, the island's mighty backbone

Santa Cruz de Tenerife – Candelaria – Arafo – Güimar – Izaña – La Esperanza – (80km/49 miles) *See map on page 64–5*

The volcanic 'backbone' of Tenerife, the so-called Cumbre Dorsal, extends from the ancient crater of Teide to the high plateau of La Laguna. Its eastern section, which is covered with pine forest, is ideal for lengthy hikes through the sweet forest air. There are also numerous observation points (*miradores*) offering a whole series of stunning views of both coasts and also of Gran Canaria on the southern horizon.

The quickest way of getting out of the polluted suburbs of ★ **Santa Cruz de Tenerife** (*see Route 1, page 18*) is to take the Avenida del Tres de Mayo and then turn left on to the Autopista del Sur. Head southwest through the inhospitable-looking landscape with its factories, power stations, apartment blocks and rubbish dumps. Near Radazul there's a yachting harbour with room for 240 vessels. Keep on past Tabaiba, a dormitory town for the middle classes who work in the capital, and soon the exit to Las Caletillas comes into view.

63

Down on the coast is the whitewashed basilica of ★ **Candelaria** (daily 7.30am–1pm and 3–7.30pm). Above the main altar is a copy of the holiest and most revered item on Tenerife, the *Black Madonna of Candelaria*, the patron saint of all the Canary Islands. According to legend, years before the *Conquista* in 1392, two Guanches found a very

Candelaria: basilica and beach

The Madonna

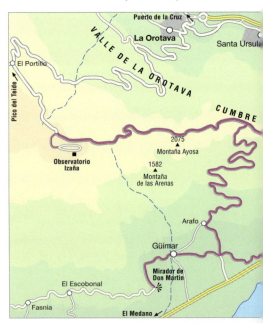

lifelike wooden Madonna, holding a child in her right arm and a candle in the other, inside a cave on the coast. When one of them touched the figure to see if was actually alive and if real blood was flowing through its veins, he accidentally cut his finger with his *tabona* (obsidian knife) and the wound began to bleed. But when he put his hand around the statue to take it to his prince, lo and behold, the wound healed instantly.

The Mencey of Güimar, who controlled the region where the Madonna was washed up, had the statue placed in a shrine and revered. When the Spanish conquerors found out about this statue and its worshippers they successfully persuaded the Mencey of Güimar that he was already halfway to Catholicism. He duly placed himself and his subjects under the control of the royal Spanish army, and in return Alonso de Lugo allowed him to play a special role after the invasion and fight at his side against the remaining Guanches in the north. The Madonna was called *Candelaria*, the 'giver of light'.

The successful conversion to Christianity of the island's 'heathens' is celebrated every summer with a pilgrimage to Candelaria. On 14 August, the eve of the Holy Mass held in honour of the Canary Islands' patron saint, the square outside the basilica fills with hundreds of pilgrims and the conversion of the Guanches is re-enacted. The high point of the solemn ceremony is the Madonna's entrance into the basilica, followed by the 'freshly' converted hea-

64

thens wearing their primeval-looking Guanche clothing and accompanied by fireworks. Finally the Plaza de la Patrona de Canarias and its surrounding streets are transformed into a seething mass of people eating, drinking, singing and making merry until the small hours.

On an ordinary day, the square outside the neo-Canarian basilica is empty. The few visitors generally wander straight past the side facing the sea, with its nine bronze Guanche princes by Canarian artist José Abad. These statues, though very detailed and realistic replacements of the original ones carved from weather-beaten volcanic rock, do have a slightly kitschy edge to them. The interior of the basilica is extremely kitschy too. This attempt at magnificence dates from 1958, and with the exception of the gentle expression of the Madonna – which is an 1830 copy by Fernando Estévez of an earlier copy in the Pilar Church in Santa Cruz – the whole place is utterly overdone.

Further on there's a narrow strip of black beach but, as it has no jetty to protect it from the open sea, it is only safe to swim here if the water is calm.

The northwestern suburb of **Las Caletillas** now has a relatively high-standard tourist infrastructure with restaurants and hotels, mostly visited by locals during the summer months. Anyone who finds the gravel-strewn beach here rather uncomfortable can always take a dip in one of the hotel pools instead.

The Guanche princes

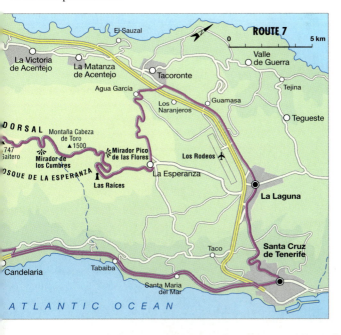

Climbing up into the hills is an assortment of terraced fields, where wine, maize, tomatoes and papaya are cultivated. These become more well-tended as we near **Arafo**, a rather sleepy village that has won several 'best-kept' prizes. An ancient Canary pine stands at the entrance to the village with a chapel next to it. Nearby is a complex on several levels with a tourist information centre, an ice-cream shop and several craft stores. At the centre of the village, the old people sit in the shade of the laurel trees in the square outside the church, and a small pavilion provides the usual snacks.

Arafo is famous throughout Tenerife for its *truchas*, a form of ravioli which was formerly only available around Christmas time. At weekends, the village awakes from its sleep and starts dancing to salsa rhythms. It holds several music and dancing events during the year and the musicians here have won several awards. Check the posters for details of forthcoming performances.

Güimar

Mirador on the Cumbre Dorsal

A worthwhile detour can be made at this point to the bustling town of ★ **Güimar**, especially to try its wines, or to enjoy the view of the Valle de Güimar, which is rather barren and dry in comparison to the Valle de Orotava (*see pages 42–3*). The best views are from the **Mirador de Don Martín** up on the Ladera on the other side of the town. It's fun guessing what the different crops are below – pineapple, avocado, banana, chirimoya, guava, cereal or wine. A layer of water-absorbent pumice can be seen spread across the ground in some places and the rich plain is punctuated by the clear outline of the Güimar volcano. A Guanche capital (*see page 15*), Güimar formed a secret alliance with the Spanish invaders which made it into a prosperous town. Around the Dominican convent, now the Town Hall, are traditional white houses and cobbled

streets, and a plaque there commemorates Isidro Quintero Acosta, a local man who introduced the cultivation of cochineal to the island. As far as the town's wines are concerned, they are improving yearly and a tasting is definitely worthwhile.

Down on the coast, at **Puerto de Güimar**, there are several places to swim. In the centre people lie on the pebble beach between the fishing boats or on the quay walls, and outside the town, in the direction of the Club Náutico, there's a grey sandy beach.

Space between the fishing boats

Back in Arafo, the road leads out of the village through a series of bends, passing black heaps of volcanic ash, until it reaches the pine forests up on the **Cumbre Dorsal**. In good weather, Gran Canaria can be seen clearly from up here. At the junction with the main road, which travels the length of this dorsal ridge, make a detour and turn left (ie southwest) to reach the brilliantly white observatories of **Izaña**. Alongside several *miradores*, with good views of Tenerife's north and south coasts, there are also some fascinating volcanic landscapes up here. At the place where the road was cut through solid rock, sections of stone have been exposed with layers reminiscent of onion skin. At another section (just before kilometre stone 32) there's a deep 'S' bend where the impressively different volcanic colours and layers are clearly visible.

Izaña observatories

Volcanic layers exposed

Izaña is basically a restricted area, but it can still be visited with permission, ideally in groups. The scientists, many of whom are very young, are often pleased to have their lonely research interrupted to show interested visitors what a sunspot looks like under magnification.

An alternative route out of Arafo is to take a right turn straight after leaving the village and enter into the peaceful and very beautiful forest known as the **Bosque de la Esperanza**. Consisting mainly of Canary pine, this large forest is ecologically essential as far as the island's water supply is concerned. The long pine needles collect water from the clouds, and the soil in the forest therefore has three times the water content of other areas. Canary pine is more resistant to forest fires because of its thick, impenetrable bark, and is also relatively impervious to extended periods of summer drought or winter frost. These advantages have finally been realised, and a great deal of reafforestation using the endemic variety has replaced the former use of other faster-growing species.

The Esperanza Forest has a whole network of footpaths and is ideal for any length of hike. In some places there are large heaps of pine needles, raked together to be taken to banana plantations to improve the thin soil there. At

Excellent riding country

weekends this forest is full of Canarian picnickers seated around barbecues, feasting away. One of these public barbecue areas is in the section of forest known as **Las Raíces**, and it was here in 1936 that General Franco and his officers cheerfully celebrated their joint opposition to the legally elected Republican government in Madrid. Franco left Tenerife on 17 July 1936 on a pretext and days later was in Morocco at the head of a small army. The die was now cast, and Spain was plunged into a bitter, three-year civil war which ended with the clerical-conservative military dictatorship under Franco's leadership. An obelisk dating from the Franco era stands in memory of the right-wing nationalist celebration here.

The village of **La Esperanza** and its environs are famous for restaurants that serve large helpings of very filling food. Pork, veal and rabbit dishes are particularly popular, as are country sausages. Beware, though, at weekends the establishments here get very crowded.

A *Tinerfeño* family called the Los Verga have also attracted much interest recently with their old Guanche combat technique, handed down through the generations. The sport is known as *el juego del palo*, and is similar to the old English quarterstaff fights. Elisio Verga, champion of the sport until his death in 1993, has now been succeeded by his sons, but his wife Luciana is particularly adept as well.

Those who failed to eat in La Esperanza should do so in **Guamasa** instead. Either side of the motorway, roads lead to the airport at Los Rodeos and to La Laguna. They are lined by a whole series of restaurants often patronised by the nearby suburbs of La Laguna and Santa Cruz. The food here is generally good, but the prices aren't particularly low.

68

A popular local restaurant

Route 8

The plantations and volcanic wastelands of the South

El Médano – Los Abrigos – Valle San Lorenzo– San Miguel – Granadilla – Arico – Fasnia – Los Roques – Poris de Abona (115km/71 miles) *See map on page 70–1*

This trip through what used to be the most inhospitable part of Tenerife is particularly recommended for lovers of unusual landscapes. At the centre of an arid, volcano-strewn wasteland, plantations, greenhouses, recreation parks and tourist centres have sprung up. The contrast between the bizarre-looking wilderness and the man-made oases of modern civilisation could not be more striking. The high road in the south, which is ideal for cycling, provides continuous views across this strangely unfinished-looking stretch of landscape.

The beach at El Médano

69

The only natural sandy beach on Tenerife is at **El Médano**, which translated means 'the dune'. However, there's not much that resembles a dune here today – it must have been buried long ago beneath the modern town. El Médano is by no means overcrowded, though, probably because it offers relatively little accommodation in comparison to the other holiday centres. The main beach has some astonishingly quiet restaurants and bars along it.

The town has made a name for itself in the international windsurfing scene. The wind conditions in the bay between the town and the Montaña Roja, formerly a volcano, have turned El Médano into one of the top ten windsurfing spots in the world. The Playa Sur Tenerife Hotel here provides everything a surfer could possibly want, and the town contains several establishments where equipment can be rented. Now that some airlines have agreed not to charge extra for windsurfing equipment, bringing one's own board and sail is more common.

Expert manoeuvres

Playa de la Tejita

Beyond the Montaña Roja is the longest natural beach on the island, the **Playa de la Tejita**. It was mainly used by locals for many years (also as a nudist beach), but these days visitors arrive here regularly in coaches from all the main tourist centres. They often bring their own music (complete with loudspeakers) and other forms of entertainment. Nevertheless, the beach is easily large enough to get away from them if you prefer peace. In fact it provides enough room for all kinds of beach activities. There's no natural shade, so sun protection is absolutely essential. There has recently been some construction work nearby, and a ban on buildings any nearer is still being supported by conservationists.

Los Abrigos

Teeing off at Golf del Sur

The next community of any size along the coast road to the south of Reina Sofía airport is the fishing village of **Los Abrigos**, which specialises in seafood restaurants. The harbour bay, surrounded by rocks, contains several seafood establishments that are very popular with the locals at weekends. Since the fishermen can hardly keep up with demand during peak season, though, beware of 'fresh-frozen' fare. The best policy is to ask the waiter what is freshly caught that day rather than simply ordering from the set menu.

The desert-like wilderness around Los Abrigos contrasts sharply with the landscape just a few miles out of town. The lush green colour of a well-tended golf course Golf del Sur (*see page 85*), with all the attendant luxuries, dominates the horizon. The road then passes several banana plantations, enclosed by very ugly walls to protect them from the wind, on the way to **Las Galletas**,

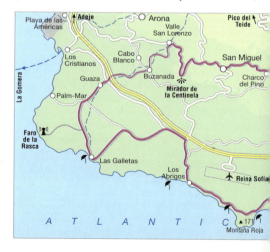

another fishing village. To the east of it are the large and self-contained holiday complexes of **Tenerife Belgica** and **Costa del Silencio**. Las Galletas itself has a narrow sand and shingle beach beyond its tiled promenade. The beach in the yacht harbour, protected by a jetty, is shingle only.

From Las Galletas, the route leads away from the sea and into the tourist-free hinterland. Just before **Guaza**, however, there's the chance to go dromedary riding. The village also boasts a Go-Kart centre, and near **Aldea Blanca** is a fake castle, where medieval banquets and jousting tournaments are held.

Irrigation technique

The valley and the very modern-looking town of ★ **Valle San Lorenzo** are situated on a section of rock that is far older even than the island's entire central massif (*see Geology and landscape, page 7*). Nevertheless, the volcanic character of the terrain is clearly visible. Thousands of small to medium-sized volcanic cones dot the terrain. The fertile soil, the high temperatures and the water supply from the massif to the north mean that conditions are ideal for growing anything that can stand the heat such as bananas, tomatoes, flowers, potatoes, and all kinds of tropical fruit.

71

The best view of this truly unusual landscape is from the ★★ **Mirador de la Centinela** on the road leading to San Miguel (C822). Suddenly, double the usual amount of volcanic cones can be seen, because the San Miguel area in many ways resembles the Valle San Lorenzo. On a clear afternoon free of haze, with the prospect of a fine sunset, this is definitely the place to come. The cones throw long shadows across the landscape, and on clear autumn evenings, the sun sets right between the islands of El Hierro and La Gomera.

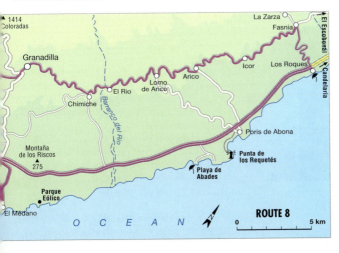

ROUTE 8

The village of **San Miguel** is mainly agricultural, and was always relatively poor. Many of its inhabitants emigrated to Cuba and Venezuela as a last resort. Today some of them have returned to live here again, having earned enough abroad to afford their own homes. The terraced fields extend far up the slopes to the pine forest layer.

Travel via **Charco el Pino**, where cochineal beetles are still scratched off their host cacti and sold to cosmetics and beverage firms (*see page 10*), to **Granadilla**, a town with an interesting mixture of old and modern buildings. Ever since the Franciscan monks decided to add an orange garden to their monastery (now dissolved), oranges have been a staple product of the local agriculture. Other crops include tomatoes, peppers, wine, maize and potatoes. The church on the way out of town was consecrated to St Anthony of Padua in 1711.

The road to Arico

Tiny house in Arico el Viejo

From Granadilla onwards, the road has a lot less traffic, but only well-trained cyclists should hazard its gradients. Motorists should certainly choose a cloudy day for the drive if possible, because it can get pretty hot. Do sound your horn very loudly before all the hairpins, and do remember to bring along enough to drink and enough sun protection. The great thing is that it's possible to take side-roads down to the coast and go for a swim at quite frequent intervals. Try to keep going as far as Villa de Arico, however, because the beaches before it are either hard to reach or not all that exciting. Along the route, terraced fields alternate with deep *barrancos*, spanned by tiny bridges. Several canals extend along the slopes, bringing the all-important water to the tourist sections of the south from as far away as the heights above Güimar.

★ **Arico** is made up of three very different sections: Villa or Lomo de Arico, Arico el Viejo and Arico el Nuevo. Villa de Arico is the largest of the three and boasts plenty of restaurants along its main street. The church, modelled after the one in Granadilla, contains a Gothic statue of the Virgin which, legend has it, was discovered on the beach near Porís de Abona. She's the patron saint of the south of the island, and attracts the odd pilgrim to this quiet village on public holidays.

★★ **Arico el Viejo** is the oldest section of town. It has an Arabian-looking church with two domed towers on the edge of a *barranco*, towering above a cluster of tiny white-washed houses. The streets are narrow and unexpectedly picturesque – it's a real village idyll.

The region around **Fasnia** is the best place on this route to spot one of the island's inhabited caves. (Note the television aerial on its 'roof'). In the mountains above Fasnia there are several small hamlets, including **La Zarza**, which can be reached along a small, winding road. The sheer amount of agricultural activity up here is quite astonishing. Not far from Fasnia is the 400-m (1,312-ft) high Montaña de Fasnia with two small white chapels on top. This volcanic hill is the ideal jumping-off point for paragliding beginners.

Those wishing to continue along the high road will soon cross a mighty *barranco* with an enormous oval stone 'flower' on its western side. On the other side, a tunnel has been built through the rock for the road. It was in this *barranco* in around 1770 that a large number of mummified Guanche corpses was discovered in a cave. Many of these finds are on display at the Archaeological Museum in Santa Cruz (*see page 21*).

Cyclists can continue along the road following the coast that goes via Güimar to Candelaria (*see page 63*) as the traffic is never very busy there. The route now turns back towards the sea. The road that goes southwards from Fasnia ends up at **Los Roques**, a tiny village in a rocky bay with two beaches. The one on the left, the Playa del Abrigo, is the larger of the two but has had a rather neglected feel to it ever since the snack stands left and a nearby construction project was announced. The smaller beach is in the middle of the village and has a sea-water swimming pool in the rock. The pool to the left of it is privately owned.

Porís de Abona lighthouse and harbour

Back on the motorway, the route heads southwest. Near Porís de Abona a large bay comes into view, with a lighthouse beyond. Now and then the odd windjammer can be seen sailing across the calm waters. At the centre of **Porís de Abona** is a beach with fishing boats. A small ladder provides access to the sea for swimmers from the new promenade. By the way, there's one very good sandy beach close to here at **Abades**, where much tourist construction activity is going on at present. There's no shade, though. The most romantic part of the beach is close to a rocky promontory at the eastern end.

Wind power at El Médano

On the way back to El Médano, the wind park known as the **Parque Eólico**, a European Union alternative energy project, comes into view, and the roads to it are well signposted. Seen close up, these large wind-driven propellers produce a rather pleasant Aeolian sound, and the whole place seems like something out of a science fiction film.

In El Médano again, the evening atmosphere can be enjoyed on one of the restaurant terraces at the beach, or at the end of the jetty. Those with any energy left can ascend the Montaña Roja to admire the sunset.

Art History

Opposite: Santa Ana in Garachico

Little remains today of the original art and culture of the Canary Islands, though the Guanches did leave their pottery skills and farming techniques. The Spanish conquerors brought Flemish paintings and the work of Moorish stonemasons and Andalusian carpenters.

Architecture

The natural sights of Tenerife are extremely impressive, and are certainly the principal interest of visitors to the island. The works of man throughout the centuries – apart from the modern hotel buildings – are generally far more modest, and appreciating them requires an eye for detail.

The finest buildings dating from the Spanish colonial era are of course the churches. Their architecture is rather simple, however, and even La Laguna's cathedral is not particularly majestic. Further inland, even the smallest village church can frequently boast a magnificent retable (shelf or frame enclosing decorated panels behind an altar). Those keen on baroque decoration and with an eye for detail will discover the odd Latin American-influenced ornament on some of the island's retables (eg the one in Tacoronte), which are rarely found on mainland Spain. The church of Santa Ana in Garachico, founded in 1548, is a good place to study the beginnings of retabular art on Tenerife.

Church of San Augustín in La Orotava

75

The mighty monastery buildings often have barred wooden balconies built on their corners. These Moorish-looking observation posts afforded monks and nuns a quick view of life in the street below and are called *azotea*. There are some particularly striking examples in La Laguna and Garachico.

The Moors were creators of the Mudéjar style. Those remaining in Spain after the Arabs had been expelled from the country converted to Catholicism but continued to decorate their buildings with geometrically based designs. On the Canary Islands, many churches and palaces boast wooden roofs build in Mudéjar style. For religious reasons, Arab artists were forbidden to include representations of living creatures in their ornamentation, so they sought inspiration in imaginative forms, with plants and geometric patterns forming the basis. Mudéjar elements can often be found on doorways and window supports, carved in the soft lava stone.

Balconies are works of art...

...and so are the doors

A particular feature of the architecture of the Canaries, not only adorning the older houses of the wealthier burghers but also the more simple country houses, are the beautifully carved wooden balconies. Probably the best examples of this can be seen in La Orotava, but there are also fine specimens in La Laguna and Garachico. Another

Patio in La Laguna

Art nouveau villa in Santa Cruz

feature is the magnificent courtyards or *patios* in the centre of the older houses. The rooms surround an open central area which is often filled with plants or flowers. The houses in the historic centre of La Orotava are good examples, and the odd noble *patio* can also be found in the old centre of La Laguna. Canarian balconies are back in fashion again with the local construction companies, and are featured on many of the island's more modern town halls and municipal buildings.

In the countryside, the odd magnificent *finca* (country estate) can be seen shining white in the midst of banana plantations with the blue sea behind it. The grey, box-shaped, concrete buildings dotted across the island are another story entirely, many of them have simply remained unfinished for tax reasons. The endless, grey walls protecting the banana plantations from the wind could also do with a more inspiring and colourful coat of paint.

Those looking for more unusual architecture should head for the capital or Las Américas, both of which boast several original hotels. Art nouveau buildings and similar can be found mostly in the Rambla quarter of Santa Cruz. In the business district, several delightful fin-de-siècle structures have unfortunately had to make way for some rather tedious modern buildings.

Painting

Geographical remoteness and the centuries of poverty of its inhabitants explain why the Canary Islands culture can boast little by way of indigenous creativity. César Manrique (1920–92), an artist who lived on Lanzerote and who was killed in an accident, is the only local artist to achieve world fame. His international reputation rests not only on his paintings and sculptures, but on his work as a nature conservationist and his battle to preserve the islands from thoughtless building schemes.

Churches and palaces which are at least 300 years old contain numerous paintings and altars by 16th- and 17th-century Flemish masters. At the time, the Netherlands formed part of the Spanish empire.

Ceramics

The legacy of the Guanches can clearly be seen in the local pottery. The art of ceramics was traditionally practised by the women and reveals definite similarities with the pottery of North Africa, pointing to a link between the North African Berbers and the Guanches. The pots were formed without a potters wheel and have no 'foot'. They were made by placing strips of black clay on top of each other and then decorating with fine, mostly naive motifs. Terracotta stamps (*pintaderas*) were used in order to print patterns on cloth.

Festivals and Folklore

Fiesta time in Puerto de la Cruz

Island customs

The most authentic customs are still probably the *paseo*, where people wander up and down the central square or main street discussing the day's events and looking around for potential partners, and the many village festivals (*fiesta*), each of which includes a solemn procession followed by much merry-making.

Village festivals usually last a week and include the weekends at either end. They begin with a religious event, when an effigy of the saint being honoured is solemnly carried through the streets. There's no shortage of firecrackers exploding during these processions, and if the events take place during the evening they are often accompanied by firework displays too. High attendances at Masses underline the religious importance of the proceedings. The real highlight of these festivals, however, are the dances held in the tinsel-bedecked church squares, with samba and salsa rhythms echoing through the streets.

Semana Santa and Corpus Christi

The highlights of the church calendar are Holy Week *(Semana Santa)* and Corpus Christi. During Holy Week, realistic sculptures depicting the Passion are carried through the streets by eerie-looking hooded figures to solemn music. Holy Week is particularly impressive in La Laguna.

Corpus Christi in June is an eight-day festival when towns rival each other with their elaborate decorations. For days beforehand enormous tableaux depicting holy scenes are created in the island's streets and squares out of flower petals and the richly-coloured volcanic sands of Las Cañadas. The most ambitious and spectacular of these compositions can be admired outside the Town Hall in La Orotava.

Folk music

Folklore is undergoing something of a revival at the moment, mainly thanks to a combination of tourist interest on the one hand and a growing awareness of Canarian regional identity on the other. Music groups in folk dress travel around the island singing and dancing at events such as *fiestas*, music contests and agricultural fairs. The dances include the slow, 18th-century *Malageña*, the more modern and definitely more cheerful *Berlina*, happy melodies (*Folía, Saltona* and *Seguidilla*) and folk songs in three-four rhythm *(Isa)*. The singing is usually accompanied by stringed instruments. The most characteristic of these is the *Timple*, a small guitar with a pronounced hump in its soundboard, which has earned it the nickname *Camelillo* (small camel).

Musical accompaniment

Canarian Carnival

Officially forbidden under Franco, the Canarian Carnival was revived in the 1980s and has gone from strength to strength. Based broadly on Mardi Gras in Rio de Janeiro, preparations are made months in advance for the processions, and the sound that is almost uninterrupted for two weeks is that of salsa and samba music. Like their Brazilian counterparts, the Canarian Carnival princesses perform great feats of strength that can sometimes very nearly wipe the smile off their faces.

The Carnival is based around a new theme each year. The time that the Plaza de España, in Santa Cruz de Tenerife, was transformed into a sight resembling the pyramids of Egypt will never be forgotten. The real high points of the Canarian Carnival are the election of the princesses, the processions through Santa Cruz on Shrove Tuesday and Puerto de la Cruz the following weekend, and also the rather foolish mock funeral of an enormous (papier-mâché) sardine, which is then burnt to cinders in the Plaza de España. All this of course accompanied by frenetic dancing in the towns' and villages' streets and squares.

It's always a tough bout

Lucha Canaria

The islanders regard *lucha Canaria* as a very masculine but also very fair sport. It's a form of wrestling in which two teams of 12 members compete against one another with just one man from each team wrestling at a time. If a wrestler remains undefeated he can take on several more opponents in a row. Each encounter consists of a maximum of three rounds, and the winner is the one who fells his opponent twice within the designated circle, receiving a point for his team. 'Felling' here means forcing him to touch the ground with any part of his body other than his feet. These wrestling matches are held during the first half of the year, but also take place during the festivals.

Festival calendar

January 5/6: In Santa Cruz on the 5th, the **Calbagata del los Reyes Magos** celebrates the coming of the Three Kings with a colourful procession. The following day, **Epiphany**, is the day on which Spanish children finally get their Christmas presents.

End of February/beginning of March: Carnival is celebrated all over the island, but especially in Santa Cruz and Puerto de la Cruz (*see page 78*).

Easter: Processions are held all over the island during **Holy Week** (*Semana Santa*). The most impressive is in La Laguna.

May: the beginning of the month heralds the start of the **Fiestas de Primavera** (Spring Festivals) in Santa Cruz.

June: Corpus Christi processions, especially worth seeing in La Laguna and La Orotava (*see page 77*). The end of Corpus Christi marks the beginning of the *roméria* season, local fiestas with an agricultural flavour. The **Roméria de San Isidro** in La Orotava (mid-June) and the **Roméria de San Benito** in La Laguna (late June or early July) are two of the largest and best attended.

July: In the week around the 15th, Puerto de la Cruz holds its **Fiesta de la Virgen del Carmen**, a lively extravaganza with nautical games and regattas centred on its old fishing harbour. There are numerous festivals honouring local patron saints, eg in La Laguna.

August 14–15: Pilgrimage and fiesta in honour of the patroness of the Canarian archipelago, **Nuestra Señora de la Candelaria**. The square around the basilica in Candelaria is packed with thousands of devotees. **16**: **Romeria de San Roque** in Garachico. **25**: Santa Cruz celebrates the city's victory over Nelson.

September: Festival of Milenario in Icod de los Vinos. The **Fiestas del Santísimo Cristo** in La Laguna and Tacoronte coincide with the grape harvest. There are cattle shows and displays of *lucha Canaria*, as well as fireworks and a veteran car rally around the island.

December 8: **Immaculada Concepción** (Immaculate Conception. **24**: Firework displays after Christmas mass. **28**: **Día de los Inocentes** (Day of the Holy Innocents) is the Spanish equivalent of April Fool's Day. **31**: New Year is greeted with firework displays and celebrations all over the island.

Fiesta de la Virgen del Carmen

Food and Drink

Like most places that have to cater to hordes of foreign tourists, the Canary Islands basically have two types of cuisine, an international one tailored to the assumed needs and expectations of other countries – which ranges from inexpensive and inedible to expensive and overpriced, though one can be lucky – and true Canarian cuisine, which usually has to be looked for inland. The search is well worth the effort.

Traditional cooking

Canary Island cuisine is very filling. One of its main-stays is the *puchero*, a hearty stew containing up to seven different kinds of meat, tomato, carrots, onions, chickpeas and salt, with cabbage, pumpkin, beans and sweet pota-toes cooked apart and added only at the moment of serv-ing. The whole dish is spiced with crushed garlic, pepper, cloves and olive oil. All the ingredients arrive in a large pot and a section of *chorizo*, a spicy sausage, can also be added for good measure.

Leisure time well spent

Local cheeses

81

Another real speciality is marinated rabbit with sea-salt potatoes and *mojo* sauce. The marinade consists of gar-lic, parsley, oregano, thyme, paprika, pepper, salt, olive oil and vinegar. The rabbit is left in it overnight and then stewed in a ceramic pot over a wood fire, while being sprinkled regularly with wine. The most popular side dish with this meal consists of *papas arrugadas* – whole pota-toes left in their jackets and boiled in a small quantity of sea water to give them a salty outer crust, and the famous *mojo* sauce. Every good restaurant will have its own ver-sion of this sauce, which comes in two colours, either red or green. The red one (*mojo rojo*) contains saffron, cumin and chilli, while the green one (*mojo verde*) is flavoured with parsley or coriander.

The sea-salt potato and *mojo* sauce combination also works exceptionally well as a side dish for seafood. All the coastal resorts have delicious fresh fish – just ask the waiter what he can recommend.

Canarian desserts are no less delicious. Try *turrón de gofio*, a pastry made of almonds, honey, maize and figs; *bienmesabe*, a soufflé of egg and almonds; or *frangollo*, a sweet pudding made of maize and milk. *Gofio* is wheat or barley, or a mixture of the two, which has been roasted before being ground. It was the staple diet of the origi-nal inhabitants of the Canary Islands and still forms an es-sential part of the diet today.

Canarian drinks

Café solo (the Canarian version of an *espresso*) is drunk after a meal to aid digestion, but a *café cortado* (*espresso*

Just the place for a café solo

Bar in Santa Cruz

with milk added) is somewhat gentler. *Café con leche* is ordinary coffee with milk. Favourite alcoholic beverages include a banana liqueur produced on the island, and also a sweet honeyed rum called *ron miel*. Rum can be obtained pure as well as in all kinds of different versions. Another popular drink is the home-made spirit known as *aguardiente de barra*. Local beer is tasty, and not too strong.

For mere thirst-quenching, try the local mineral water (direct from Mount Teide), and all the different fruit juice variations. One delicious milk shake is the light-green, creamy *Batido de Aguacate* (avocado milkshake).

Island wines

Fruits of the vine

The Canaries' traditional wines are an acquired taste. Made from the *malvasia* grape and grown on volcanic soil, their flavour is often reminiscent of sherry. The boom in tourism and a growing interest in locally made produce recently prompted the wine-growers of northeastern Tenerife to club together and form the vintners' association of Tacoronte-Acentejo.

Tenerife's wines can be found in many of the island's supermarkets. *Viña Norte* is produced by Bodegas Insulares, SA and is a popular wine. Getting hold of a red *Gran Tinerfe* from Matanza de Acentejo is far harder, since only 7,000 bottles are produced annually. The wines are almost always a mixture of two or three different grape varieties. The white wines are usually a blend of Listán Blanco, Malvasía and Gual, and the reds a mixture of Listán Negro and Negramoll.

Restaurant selection

These suggestions for restaurants in some of the most popular spots are listed according to the following price categories: $$$ = expensive; $$ = moderate; $ = inexpensive.

El Tanque
$$El Medio Oriente, Carretera General, tel: 830729, meat, fish, quail, good *mojo* sauces; **$$La Llovizna**, Principes de España, tel: 831300, tasty chicken dishes; **$Monte Verde**, Principes de España 10, tel: 830902, excellent *puchero*.

Garachico
$$$Isla Baja, Esteban de Ponte 5, tel: 830008, good but very expensive; **$Princesa Dacil**, Eutropio Rodriquez de la Sierra 2, tel: 830302, delicious seafood.

Guamasa
$$$Los Limoneros, in Los Naranjeros near the Carretera General del Norte, tel: 636637, international food with regional specialities, excellent wines.

La Esperanza
$$Casa Manolo, Salto de Pino 32, Llano del Moro, tel: 610091, famous for its cooked goat.

Los Abrigos
$$Perlas del Mar, La Marina, tel: 176414, out on a rock in the sea; **$$Vista Mar**, Avenida Maritima, tel: 176156, tasty paella; **$Langostera**, Paseo Maritimo, tel: 176319.

Los Abrigos awaits custom

Los Realejos
$$$Villa Nueva, San Vincente, Princesa Dasil 31, tel: 341558, closed Wednesday, Canarian cuisine; **$$$Las Chozas**, El Jardin, La Carrera 64, tel: 432054, excellent lobster and sole; **$$El Monasterio**, La Montañeta 12, tel: 340707, inside former monastery rooms, try the chicken in marjoram sauce.

Masca
$$La Pimentera, tel: 863438, tasty food and good view; **$La Fuente**, tel: 863466, closed Friday, terrace with view; **$Casa Enrique - Chez Arlette**, tel: 863459, closed Saturday, flowery terrace; **$El Guanche**, tel: 863424, Canarian food, flowery terrace, half-board also available.

A meal in Masca

Puerto de la Cruz
$$$Casino Taoro, tel: 380550, international; **$$$Magnolia**, Urbanisación La Paz, tel: 385614, international; **$$La Papaya**, Lomo 10, tel: 382811, fax: 387796, closed Wednesdays, Canarian cuisine, attractive patio; **$El Regulo**, San Felipe 16, Canarian cooking; **$Tropical**, Lomo 7, tel: 385312, fresh fish.

Popular Puerto de la Cruz

San Andrés
$$Ramon, Dique 23, tel: 549308, fresh shrimps and fish from the bay; **$$El Rubi**, Dique 19, tel: 549673, fish and also paella; **$La Langostera**, Avenida Maritima, tel: 549006, delicious seafood, freshly caught, probably the best food in town.

Santa Cruz
$$$Cafeteria Olympo, Plaza de la Candelaria 1, tel: 241738, Spanish and Canarian cuisine; **$$$Da Gigi**, Avenida Anaga 43, tel: 242017/284607, Italian food; **$$La Lateria**, Benavides 30, tel: 249778, Canarian cuisine; **$Viva Mexico**, Avenida de Madrid, tel: 205805, Mexican; **$Tasca Tshing**, 25 de Julio 26, tel: 285978, Chinese; **$El Zaguan**, Parque Viera y Clavijo, creperie.

Tacoronte
$$Las Cuevas de Tacoronte, Carretera General del Norte 165, El Cantillo, tel: 560000, Canarian cuisine.

Sunset over Puerto de la Cruz

Nightlife

As everywhere in Southern Europe much of the nightlife in Tenerife takes place on the streets. Canary Islanders need no clubs to find entertainment at night. Spontaneous chats in the squares and on the beaches, and dance music spilling out on to the pavements from the bars are commonplace, and holidaymakers can join in the fun.

There are plenty of nightclubs and discos primarily in the tourist hotspots, and very little starts before midnight. Here is a selection:

Night lights in La Américas

Las Américas
Prismas, Paseo Maritime, near the Tenerife Sol hotel; **Melody**, near the Pueblo Canario; **Trauma**, near the Centro Comercial Palm Beach.

Los Realejos
Coco Loco, near the Hotel Maritim.

Puerto de la Cruz
Victoria and Royal, Avenida Colon; **Joy**, Obispo Perez Caceres; **Concordia**, Avenida Venezuela; **Coto** and **Catar** in the Urbanisación La Paz.

Santa Cruz
KU, Avenida de Madrid, tel: 203636; **Salsa con Gofio**, **Big Bang**, and **Pachaalso**, three open-air discos in the harbour area to the south.

Gambling
The Casino Taoro in Puerto de la Cruz is probably one of the best casinos in Europe, tel: 380550/300666. There is also a casino in Plaza Candelaria in Santa Cruz.

Active Holidays

Tenerife has a vast range of sports possibilities for the athletically or adventurously inclined. Many hotels have their own keep-fit programmes as well.

Diving

Most of the diving schools on Tenerife are situated in the southwest of the island. Those keen to know more should contact Jean and Annie Koller at the Costa del Silencio near Las Galletas (tel: 730060, fax: 730981), the diving school in the Hotel Palmeras in Las Américas (tel: 790991) or the Baracuda Diving School in the Hotel Paraíso Floral on the Playa Paraíso, near Las Américas (tel: 780725).

Sailing

There are several harbours from where you can sail, including Radazul (tel: 615458 or 610550), Los Gigantes (tel: 101601) and Los Cristianos (tel: 791102).

At anchor off Los Cristianos

Windsurfing

Ideal conditions at El Médano

Many tourist centres provide windsurfing lessons and El Médano (*see Route 8, page 69*) is the best place for enthusiasts to head for.

Golf

There's a good 18-hole course in La Laguna. For more information contact Campo de Golf, Los Rodeos, tel: 630115. There's also the Golf del Sur course near Los Abrigos, with 27 holes, tel: 785058, fax: 785272.

Hang-gliding

This is a very popular sport on Tenerife, and there are courses available, for beginners and the more experienced, at the Parapente Club del Sur, Edificio Esmeralda 39, Callao Salvaje, tel: 781357.

Hiking

Those interested in going on organised hikes have several options. The Teide National Park administration provides a free introduction to the island's flora and fauna twice a week, and this is combined with a hike through Las Cañadas (after a bus trip to get there). Those travelling by bus in Las Cañadas should check when the last one leaves the stop at the Parador Nacional hotel. For more information contact the Visitor Centre at El Portillo or tel: 259903 or 263898. The Tigaiga Hotel (tel: 383500) in Puerto de la Cruz also organises hikes with varying degrees of difficulty. For guided hiking trips through the mountains contact the Hotel Paraíso Floral at Las Américas (tel: 780725).

Getting There

By air

Flights to Tenerife in peak season should always be booked in good time – up to at least six months in advance to be on the safe side – Reina Sofía Airport in the south is one of the busiest airports in the Canaries. Scheduled and charter flights are frequent. These are usually part of a package which includes accommodation, so travel agencies can provide all the necessary information. In summer there are many direct flights to Tenerife from the UK and the USA. It is also possible to fly from international airports around the world and pick up a domestic flight there. Spain's national airline Iberia provides regular services to Tenerife from most major European cities.

Opposite: Zigzags up the Masca Valley

Reina Sofía Airport

By sea

If you are travelling by ship you will reach Tenerife on the ferry run by the national steamship company Compañia Trásmediterranea. The voyage from Cadiz on mainland Spain to Tenerife departs every Saturday arriving on the Monday. Although the ferry has a pool and various restaurants on board, the trip is by no means a joy ride (there is no entertainment programme, and the sea is often rough).
In the UK: Southern Ferries, 179 Piccadilly, London W1V 9DB, tel: 0171-491 4968.
In Spain: Calle Obenque 4, 28042 Madrid, tel: 322 9100.
On Tenerife: Estacion Marito Muelle Ribera, Santa Cruz de Tenerife, tel: 287850.

87

Island-hopping

Flying between the Canary Islands themselves is almost as easy as catching a bus. Iberia's Binter Canaria airline runs half-hourly flights to the islands, so generally you don't have to book in advance, although around Christmastime and other Canarian *fiesta* holidays it may be advisable to book to be on the safe side.

The inter-island air traffic is handled by the Los Rodeos Airport near La Laguna. Further information may be obtained from the Aeropuerto Tenerife Norte (Los Rodeos), tel: 257745, or in Santa Cruz de Tenerife, Avenida de Anaga 23, tel: 333111 or 333222. For reservations in the UK, tel: 0171-830 0011.

Information on boat connections between the islands can be obtained from Compañia Trásmediterranea (*see above*). The Ferry Gomera also connects with La Gomera and is run by Fred Olsen Lines. Further information available from Fred Olsen S.A. Dr Zerolo 14, Santa Cruz de Tenerife, tel: 282062. The car ferry to Gran Canaria takes four hours for the 63-km (39-mile) crossing. The jetfoil is quicker (80 minutes).

Ferry to La Gomera

Getting Around

By bus

Tenerife has a comprehensive bus network covering the entire island. TITSA, the largest bus company, serves all the major towns and communities several times a day. Its timetables may be obtained from the larger bus stations, such as those at Santa Cruz or La Laguna. Ask about special offers. There are other, smaller bus companies apart from TITSA which serve the more remote communities.

There is a regular bus service running from Reina Sofia Airport in the south to Santa Cruz which is linked to scheduled flights from mainland Spain.

In Santa Cruz de Tenerife, the bus station is located on the Avenida Tres de Mayo. The terminus for the bus connecting with La Laguna is on the Bravo Murillo. Those headed for Las Terestitas should board their bus at the sea promenade north of the Plaza de España.

In Puerto de la Cruz, the main bus station is on the Calle de Pozo. Las Américas is connected by bus to all the beaches in the south and southwest from El Médano, Las Galletas and Los Cristianos as far as Los Gigantes. There are also direct connections to Santa Cruz de Tenerife and to Puerto de la Cruz via Las Cañadas. La Laguna has TITSA and Transmersa buses. The latter are particularly useful for hikers eager to penetrate the Anaga. For more information, contact the large bus station near the Los Rodeos airport turn-off on the Autopista del Norte.

Taxis are quite cheap

By taxi

Taxis on Tenerife are relatively cheap. Make sure you settle on the price beforehand, however. For cross-island trips it's best to consult the list of fixed prices.

Car rental

Tenerife has 100 different car companies, all vying for custom, so you are in a position to shop around. The longer you are wanting the car, the better the rate. Vehicles from the larger rental firms can be booked before your trip and picked up at the airport on arrival.

Slow down at the bends

Traffic regulations

Tenerife basically has the same highway code as elsewhere in Europe. At roundabouts, cars coming from the right have priority unless otherwise indicated. One interesting local rule is that you should indicate any intention of slowing down or stopping (because of any obstacle etc) to the driver behind by using your left indicator or by sticking out your left hand. On long stretches of mountain road with blind curves it's always best to sound your horn before going round them.

Index

La Orotava
$$Parador de Turismo Las Cañadas del Teide, Apartado de Correos 15, tel: 386415, fax: 232503; **$Pension Silene**, Tomas Zerolo 9, tel: 330199.

Las Americas
$$$Jardin Tropical, Urbanización San Eugenio, tel: 794111, fax: 794451; **$$Torviscas Playa**, Urbanisación Torviscas, tel: 797300, fax: 797470.

Los Cristianos
$$$Mediterranean Palace, Avenida del Litoral, tel: 794400, fax: 793622; **$$Oasis Moreque**, tel: 790366, fax: 792260; **$Marino**, Chayofita 10, tel: 795517; **$Reveron**, General Franco 26, tel: 790600; **$La Paloma**, San Juan XXIII, tel: 790198.

Los Gigantes
$$$Los Gigantes, Flor de Pascua 12, Los Gigantes, tel: 101020, fax: 100475.

Los Realejos
$$$Maritim, El Burgado 1, tel: 342012, fax: 342109; **$$Romantica I**, Bouganvilla 1, tel: 3432 1; **$Reforma**, Tierra de Oro, tel: 341213.

Puerto de la Cruz
$$$Monopol, Quintana 15, tel: 384611, fax: 370310; **$$$Melia Botanico**, Richard Yeoward s/n, tel: 381400, fax: 381504; **$$$Tigaiga**, Parque de Taoro, tel: 383500, fax: 384055; **$$Marquesa**, Quintana 11, tel: 383151, fax: 386950; **$$Condesa**, Quintana 13, tel: 381050, fax: 386950; **$$Tropical**, Plaza del Charco 9, tel: 383113; **$$Finca Ventoso**, Las Dehesas 73, tel: 383820; **$Arosa**, Triarte 21, tel: 384237; **$Puerto Azul**, Lomo 24, tel: 383213; **$Liberia**, Cruz Verde 4, tel: 383688.

Punta del Hidalgo
$$Oceano, Paseo Maritimo, tel: 541108.

Santa Cruz
$$$Mencey, Doctor Jose Navéiras 38, tel: 276700, fax: 280017; **$$Atlantico**, Castillo 12, tel: 246375; **$$Oceano**, Castillo 8, tel: 270800; **$$Plaza**, Plaza de la Candelaria 9, tel: 246862, fax: 247278; **$$Nautico**, Profesor Peraza de Ayala 13, tel: 247066, fax: 247276; **$Horizonte**, Santa Rosa de Lima 11, tel: 271936; **$Mova**, San Martin 33, tel: 283261.

Vilaflor
$German, Santo Domingo 1, tel: 709028.

95

Hotel Monopol

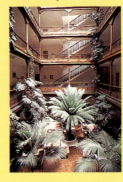

Accommodation

For over a generation there has been an enormous boom in hotel and holiday home construction on Tenerife, with no end in sight. The southwest of the island in particular is having its coastal regions steadily flooded by new hotels, some of them built high up on the bare slopes. Much of the accommodation is thus medium to high quality, but is also very much geared towards package tourism. Travellers arriving in Tenerife on their own without advance bookings will find a limited range of places to stay during peak season (ie Christmas, Easter, summer and autumn holidays), and it's by no means easy to find a cheap and suitable place to stay in the busy towns. Accommodation outside the centres usually consists of second houses or retirement homes rented out by Northern Europeans. The best way of gaining access to these is either via connections, or newspaper advertisements.

If you want to look for your own accommodation in Tenerife, the tourist offices provide lists of hotels, boarding houses and apartments with their respective price categories. Note that the categories refer only to furnishings, and not to friendly service or atmosphere – a five-star establishment just means that it's very well-furnished.

Hotel selection

These suggestions for hotels in some of the most popular spots are listed according to the following price categories: $$$ = expensive; $$ = moderate; $ = inexpensive.

Bajamar
$$Atlantic, Avenida de las Piscinas 2, tel: 543311; **$$Delfin**, Avenida del Sol, tel: 540200.

Candelaria
$$$Punta del Rey, tel: 501899, fax: 500091; **$$Tenerife Tour**, tel: 500200, fax: 502363.

El Médano
$$Playa Sur Tenerife, tel: 176120, fax: 176337; **$$Médano**, tel: 704000, fax: 176048; **$Carel**, Avenida de los Principes 22, tel: 176066, fax: 176828.

Garachico
$Francisco Hernández Delgado, Simon de Herrera 4, tel: 831076.

La Laguna
$$$Nivaria, Plaza del Adelantado 11, tel: 264298, fax: 259634,; **$$Aguere**, Obispo Rey Redondo 57, tel: 259490; **$Ramos**, Heraclio Sanchez 6, tel: 254249.

There is a good variety of hotels

Bookshops
Those looking for good, detailed information on the Canary Islands in English are advised to visit the Librería Barbara in Los Cristianos, Juan Pablo Abril 36, tel: 792301. In Santa Cruz, two good establishments are the Librería Goytec, Pérez Galdos 15, tel: 245314, and La Isla, Robayna 2, tel: 246379.

Nudism
Topless bathing has become almost the norm at swimming pools and beaches, but full nudism is still quite rare and only tolerated on particular beaches such as La Tejita (near El Médano), La Caleta (near Las Américas) and Las Gaviotas (near San Andrés).

Medical assistance
Tenerife has a large number of doctors, almost all of whom speak English, particularly in the tourist centres. Chemists (Monday to Friday 9am–1pm and 4–8pm, Saturday 9am–1pm) are recognisable by the green or red Maltese cross on the sign outside. The smaller villages usually have a first-aid station run by the Red Cross (*Cruz Roja*). In the larger towns there will always be at least one chemist open at night.

Use the sun-shades

Emergencies
There are numbers common to all the Canary Islands:
Police: tel: 091
Medical emergencies: tel: 222222.
In addition there are specific numbers to call for Tenerife:
Red Cross (*Cruz Roja*): Santa Cruz de Tenerife, tel: 281800; Puerto de la Cruz, tel: 383812; Adeje (for Las Américas), tel: 780759.
Police in the Adeje area: tel: 797811.

Crime
Pickpockets, confidence tricksters and car thieves are usually busiest in the larger towns and tourist centres, but even if you leave your (rental) car in isolated spots, eg Las Cañadas, never leave anything inside it. It's a good idea to leave the glove compartment open to prove that there really is nothing inside. In the larger tourist centres, keep your money and valuables in the hotel safe.

If the worst happens, a police report issued by the Guardia Civil will be required in order to substantiate an insurance claim.

Diplomatic representation
For the UK: Plaza de Weyler 8, 1st Floor, Santa Cruz, tel: 286863.
For the US: Alvarez de Lugo 10, Santa Cruz, tel: 286950.

Postal services

Stamps (*sellos*) can be bought at tobacconists (*tabacos*), souvenir shops selling postcards and hotel reception desks. Spanish letterboxes are yellow. All letters and postcards from the Canaries go by air and mail takes at least five days to reach Northern Europe.

Telephone

International calls can be made from public telephones marked *internacional* using 100-Pta coins, but phone cards (*tarjetas de telefónica*), available from all tobacconists and post offices, are far more practical. First dial 07, wait for the tone, then dial the rest of the code for the country you want (ie for the UK dial 07-44; US 07-1), followed by the city code (minus its initial zero) and then the actual number itself.

For international directory information, dial 025, and 003 for local information.

Time

As the Canary Islands use GMT, there is no time difference to the UK, so they are one hour behind the rest of Europe. Summer Time (GMT + one hour) also applies during the summer.

Electricity

The tourist centres almost always have 220v sockets. Voltage can vary from 110v to 125v however, and sometimes adapters are needed.

Clothing

Along with the usual summer holiday clothing, if you are planning to hike in the mountains, bring sturdy walking boots, an anorak and sweatshirt as sudden changes in weather are commonplace. In the winter, evenings are cooler, so its advisable to pack a jumper or cardigan. Bare legs and shoulders are frowned upon in churches.

No shortage of subjects

Photography

There's a vast assortment of photographic material and equipment available in the Canary Islands, and prices are around the same as those in Europe. Many of the tourist centres have overnight development services too.

Newspaper kiosk

Newspapers

In the tourist centres along the south coast, English newspapers are usually available on the day of issue. The main European newspapers and magazines can be purchased at the kiosks in the tourist centres. English-language publications about what's on in Tenerife are *Here & Now*, *The Island Gazette* and *The Holiday Magazine*.

Public Holidays

Spain not only has national holidays but regional and local ones, too, so you might find all the shops in one village closed, while in the next town it's business as usual. The following holidays are observed on the island: 1 January (*Año Nuevo*), 6 January (*Los Reyes*), 19 March (*San José*), 1 May (*Día del Trabajo*), 30 May (*Día de Canarias*), 25 July (*Santiago*), 15 August (*Asunción*), 25 August (*Derrota de Nelson*), 12 October (*Día de la Hispanidad*), 1 November (*Todos los Santos*), 6 December (*Día de la Constitución*), 8 December (*Immaculada Concepción*), 25 December (*Navidad*).

Moveable feast days are at Easter and Corpus Christi.

Shopping and souvenirs

The Canary Islands were scheduled to lose their status as a free trade (duty-free) zone by 1996, so the savings on items such as tobacco, spirits, perfume, cosmetics, watches, jewellery, electronic and optical equipment may no be longer as great as they once were.

Bargaining is expected in the flea markets and at streetside stands run by the North African merchants, but beware of 'special offers' from these traders whose goods include ivory jewellery or leather or fur goods from endangered species. Not only will you be supporting the extermination or rare animals, but the import of such items into Europe and the US is forbidden and subject to heavy penalties.

Typical Canary Island products are ceramics and embroidery, with tablecloths and cushion covers with detailed patterns a speciality. It's advisable to buy from a shop rather than a street seller though, or you may find that your souvenir was made in Taiwan.

Cigars and ceramics

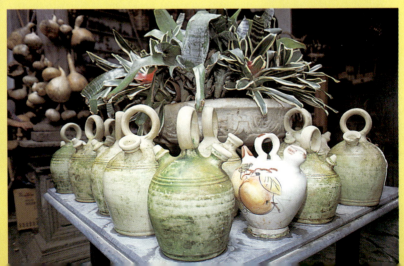

Parque Nacional del Teide

Tourist information

In the UK: Spanish Tourist Office, 57–58 St James's Street, London SW1A 1LD, tel: 0171-499 0901. For brochures, tel: 0891 669920.

In the US: Tourist Office of Spain, 665 Fifth Avenue, New York NY 10022, tel: 212-759 8822; 8383 Wilshire Blvd, Suite 960, Beverly Hills, Ca 90211, tel: 213-658 7188.

On Tenerife: Oficina de Información Turística, at Palacio Insular, Plaza de España, Santa Cruz de Tenerife, tel: 605592, and in Puerto de la Cruz at Plaza de la Iglesia 3, tel: 386000, as well as in the main tourist resorts.

Currency and exchange

The official unit of currency on Tenerife is the Spanish peseta (Pta). There are 10,000, 5,000, 2,000 and 1,000 Pta banknotes, and 500, 200, 100, 50, 25, 10, 5, 2 and 1 Pta coins. The 5-Pta coin is known familiarly as a *duro*.

The banks will exchange cash, Eurocheques (maximum amount 25,000 Ptas per cheque) and traveller's cheques but check the service charges first, as these can vary from bank to bank. Hotels and currency exchange outlets can also change money outside banking hours, but hotel rates in particular are usually unfavourable. In remote places you will probably have to present your passport when cashing a Eurocheque. In towns and holiday complexes credit cards and cash dispensers are widely used.

Tipping

In bars and restaurants the service charge is generally included in the bill, but even where prices are inclusive it is usual to tip waiters and also taxi drivers an extra 10 percent or so. Porters should get 50–100 Ptas for each piece of luggage they carry. It is also a good idea to tip hairdressers, chambermaids and room service attendants at least 100 Ptas, and the same goes for tour guides and bus drivers on excursions and round trips. When paying for drinks in cash, leave at least some peseta coins on the counter.

Late-night opening

Opening times

Shops on Tenerife have no fixed opening and closing times, though the general rule is: Monday to Friday 9am–1pm and 4–8pm, Saturday 9am–2pm. These times are much more flexible in the main tourist centres, especially in peak season, when many shops are open on Sunday as well.

Banks are open Monday to Friday 9am–2pm and Saturday 9am–1pm.

Post office (*correo*) opening times are Monday to Saturday 9am and 1pm. The main post office in Santa Cruz de Tenerife is open all hours.

Facts for the Visitor

On the road

Travel documents

Visitors from European Union countries, the Common-wealth and the United States must have a valid passport. No visa is required by nationals of the EU, Australia, Canada and New Zealand for a stay of up to three months, or by US nationals for a stay of up to six months. Visitors bringing their own car will need the vehicle registration documents and a green insurance certificate. National driving licences are accepted in the case of visitors staying less than six months on the island.

Customs

There are now no limits to the amounts of goods imported from one European Union country to another, provided they are for personal use and have been purchased in an EU country. However, the customs authorities have issued a list of maximum amounts of alcholic drinks, tobacco goods, perfumes, etc. For those coming direct from a country outside the EU, the allowances for any such goods are: 200 cigarettes or 100 cigarillos or 50 cigars or 250g tobacco; 1 litres spirits or 2 litres fortified wine or 3 litres table wine; 60cc perfume; 250cc toilet water.

The status of free-trade zone that has benefited the islands so much in the past is under threat from the EU and is likely to be phased out by 1996.

Currency and exchange

Unlimited amounts of foreign currency can be brought into the country. If the sum exported exceeds Ptas 500,000 it must be declared. Spanish currency can be imported in unlimited amounts and exported in amounts of up to Ptas 1 million per person without declaration.